Christmas SPOKEN HERE

JOHN KILLINGER

1989

BROADMAN PRESS
Nashville, Tennessee

© Copyright 1989 ● Broadman Press
All rights reserved
4222-69
ISBN: 0-8054-2269-2
Dewey Decimal Classification: 252.61
Subject Heading: CHRISTMAS - SERMONS
Library of Congress Catalog Card Number: 88-29314
Printed in the United States of America

Unless otherwise stated, Scripture quotations are from the Revised
Standard Version of the Bible, copyrighted 1946, 1952, © 1971, 1973.
Scripture quotations marked (JB) are excerpts from *The Jerusalem
Bible*, copyright © 1966 by Darton, Longman and Todd, Ltd. and
Doubleday and Company, Inc. Used by permission of the publisher.
Scripture quotations marked (KJV) are from the King James Version
of the Bible. Scripture quotations marked (NEB) are from *The New
English Bible*. Copyright © The Delegates of the Oxford University
Press and the Syndics of the Cambridge University Press, 1961, 1970.
Reprinted by permission.

Library of Congress Cataloging-in-Publication Data

Killinger, John.
  Christmas spoken here / John Killinger.
    p.   cm.
  ISBN 0-8054-2269-2
  1. Christmas sermons. 2. Sermons, American. I. Title.
BV4257.K5   1989
252'.61—dc19   88-29314
                                                             CIP

School of Divinity

Gardner-Webb University
School of Divinity

Christmas Spoken Here

Introduction

Christmas is the most heartwarming time of the year. Even self-styled agnostics or atheists bask in its glow. As for Christians, they are almost beside themselves with joy and wonder!

It is a time of incarnation, when the greatest truths of Christian preaching are embedded in song and festival and tradition. It is a time when plays, parties, carolings, and worship services all blend together into a single feast of the spirit, all focused on the innkeeper's stable in Bethlehem.

It is a time when little drummer boys play for the baby Jesus and animals are given the power of speech to praise His name, when the singing of angels is heard over barren fields and chimes sound in the night because of a child's small gift laid upon the altar.

It is a time when coldhearted Scrooges are converted and families are reborn in gentleness and caring. It is a time of uplift and excitement, when the entire human community seems to flow together in a mood of tenderness and generosity.

It is a time when God's love is more tangible than at any other time of the year, made manifest in the words of the gospel and on the faces of all the children on earth.

The preacher who cannot be understood at Christmas will have a hard time at any other season, for hearts are uncommonly open then to receive the message of salvation. The candlelight, the greenery, the warm memories, and general sense of expectancy, all make us susceptible to hearing a word from God, even if it be spoken by a lisping human voice.

The sermons in this book are hopefully such a word. Stammering, broken, incomplete, they are nevertheless the bearers of a wonderful announcement, that God has taken the principal role in the drama of redemption and is acting it out in the most incredible location—right under our very noses.

I make no mighty claims for the sermons. They are the meager offerings I set before my own congregation over a period of four or five Christmases.

But perhaps, like the scattered bits of a broken tree ornament, they will reflect—for those who have eyes to see—the resplendent glory of the God who made His habitation in a manger and continues even now to bless such lowly places.

Contents

1

Christmas Spoken Here

I was staring through the window of a beautiful little Christmas shop in Washington state. It was packed with Christmas items, even though Christmas was still six months away. There were exquisite creche scenes from Italy, Germany, and Norway. There were fuzzy-faced elves and jolly old Santa Clauses, sleighs and reindeer of every size and description, bells and trees, and music boxes. There were nutcrackers and candles and electric lights, angels and wise men and little drummer boys, stars and snowmen and gingerbread cutouts. The little shop was fairly bursting with Christmas, and a loudspeaker broadcast a medley of Yuletide tunes. It was infectious, even in the summertime. And down in the corner of the front door, where no one could miss it, was the neatest touch of all. It was a small sign that said: "Christmas Spoken Here."

"Christmas Spoken Here." I cannot imagine a

better slogan for the church, at this or any time of year, than that one. What could say better why we are here? God has entered human history to change its course forever. He has come as a Word, as something said, articulated, put in a message: "The Word became flesh and dwelt among us" (John 1:14). We remember the event each year in song and pageant and decoration. "Christmas spoken here." It has to be spoken here, for it is the basis of all we do.

Perhaps it will enhance our sense of Christmas to remember the kind of Word that came among us, that was spoken once and for all into the human arena, that is the basis for all our own speaking.

"The Word became flesh and dwelt among us." That is, it was *an intelligible Word*. It was a Word we could understand because it was like us. Suppose God had revealed himself in a riddle or in some language human beings did not speak. We would have been no better off than before, would we?

Once Anne and I traveled with an English couple from Gatwick airport into London. They had just returned from Spain where they had a harrowing experience. They had planned to board a northbound train from Barcelona. But, not understanding a word of Spanish, they got mixed up and boarded a southbound train. An hour later, a porter looked at their tickets and accused them of trying to cheat the railway company. He demanded money for extra fare, and they didn't have enough. A policeman was called, and at the next town they were taken to the police station. They had visions of spending ten years in a Spanish jail, unable to communicate with their captors. Finally an interpreter was called in, and they explained their predicament. They were placed on a northbound train and sent on their way. "We'll not go back there again!" swore the Englishman.

Suppose God had spoken to us in a language we could not understand?

But He didn't. God spoke to us in a baby, a little child born in a manger. It is a message everyone understands. Even the simple-minded understand. What more beautiful word could God have said? Flesh of our flesh, taking our nature, bearing our sins to a cross. It was a Word in the vernacular, a Word in language we can all comprehend.

I remember sitting in an international air terminal in the late afternoon. People were tired, tempers were short, and the place was a bedlam. So many languages were being spoken in the room that no one seemed to understand anyone else. Then a little child—he couldn't have been more than two or three—began toddling from party to party, touching people and smiling at everyone. People all over the room smiled as they watched him, and soon they were smiling at one another. The child had united everyone.

That is the way it is this Christmas. All over the world, people who know little of one another or one another's ways are drawn together around the figure of a child born in a manger. It is a Word we all understand, a Word of humanity and gentleness.

The Word was "full of grace and truth," said John. Unlike many words that are spoken, *it was sincere and important.* "Words are cheap," we say. That is because there are so many insincere and meaningless words in the world. I suppose it was always that way, but we have learned to reproduce them in greater quantities than any people before us, and there are times when we feel literally glutted by words.

A friend was telling me of the experience she had a few days ago. She was shopping in a department store and was passing through the TV and stereo department. A little boy, taking advantage of his parent's preoccupation in another part of the store, was turning all the TV sets to different stations. The result was a bedlam of words and messages, all blaring into the room at the same time. "I think it was a picture of modern life," said my friend, "all that speech, and none of it making any sense."

A lot of words are meaningless. But when God spoke to us that first Christmas, His Word was full of grace and truth. It was an important Word. It was a Word the whole world was waiting to hear.

There is a scene in Bernard Malamud's novel *The Fixer* that I have found deeply moving. Yakov Bok, the penniless tinkerer of the title, has been cast into prison for a murder he did not commit. Alone and friendless, he is put into solitary confinement, deep in the bowels of an ancient jail. One day another prisoner is put into the adjoining cell. The minute the new prisoner is left alone, he begins to pound against the wall with his shoe. The noise comes through distantly, and Yakov begins to pound with his own shoe. When the man shouts, Yakov can hear sound, but not words. They shout to each other at various times of the day and night as loudly as they can. It sounds to Yakov as if someone is trying to tell him a heartrending tale, and he wants to tell his own. But the man's shouts, cries, questions, are muffled, indistinguishable. Neither man can understand what the other is saying.

This, I fear, is the human predicament. We are locked in cells of fear and loneliness, and we are desperate to be in touch with someone else, to tell our stories, and hear the others, to know we are not alone. Into the midst of this awful isolation has come the most important word of all, the Word of God saying, "You are not alone,

I am with you." That is what *Emmanuel* means, isn't it? "God with us." What more important word could we hear than this one? What more important word could there be? Christmas is spoken here, and it is a Word full of grace and truth.

Finally, said John, it is a Word that has shown us the glory of God, "glory as of the only Son from the Father." What is the glory of God? In Old Testament times, it was understood as a kind of aura, a thick mist that people saw instead of seeing God Himself. No one saw God at any time; instead, they saw His glory. But the glory people saw in Jesus was more than a thick mist. It was the projection of God in His only Son, in His "only begotten Son," says the King James Version. Now, does that language remind you of anything? How about the third chapter of John? "For God so loved the world that he gave his only Son"—"his only begotten Son" (KJV)— and it goes on to talk about His dying on the cross. The real glory of God, the final glory of God, is seen in His giving His only Son to die for our sin. In other words, John meant that the Word God sent into our midst is not only a fleshly Word, a Word we can understand, and it is not only an important Word, full of grace and truth, but also *it is a loving Word*. Think about that, will you? God's Word is a loving Word, and His love reveals His true glory.

Rebecca West, the famous novelist, once sent a parcel from a store in London to a younger woman writer who was going through a bad time in her life. It contained a large bottle of perfume and an exquisite French scarf of gray-green taffeta. The card in the parcel said: "I thought you needed a bit of spoiling. Love, Rebecca."

That is the kind of word God has sent to us. We have done nothing to deserve it. In fact, we deserve very little in this world. But God has sent us a loving Word because it is God's glorious nature to love. "God is love," the Bible declares; therefore, the Word that God speaks is a word of love.

How great the glory and love of God were was not fully known at Bethlehem. It awaited that awful day at Calvary for the extent of His love to be revealed. Then it became clear: God loved us so much that He gave His only begotten Son to die on the cross.

Marc Chagall, the artist, understood. In the Musee de Chagall in the Mediterranean city of Nice hangs the great canvas of his painting of *The Sacrifice of Isaac,* a favorite theme of the Jewish painter. In the bright hues of red and blue and green for which Chagall is world famous, the painting depicts Abraham as he is about to plunge the knife into the heart of his young son Isaac. But an angel has seized his hand and holds it, and off to the side of the altar a ram has been caught by its horns in the bushes. God had provided a sacrifice to take the boy's place. Up in the corner of the painting there is another figure. It is Jesus carrying His cross to Golgotha. This is a theme to which Chagall returned again and again. It obviously preoccupied him. Jesus—*God's* Son—was not spared. Isaac, Abraham's son, was. But not God's Son. God's Son died on the cross. It was God's way of revealing His great love to the world. The child who was born in a manger grew up and died on the cross. What more could God say than this? His Word is the word of His glorious love.

"Christmas Spoken Here." It was an appropriate motto. It is an appropriate motto for us. The church ought always to speak Christmas. We ought always to be reminded of the Word God has spoken: the intelligible, important, and loving Word of His concern for us. And Christmas is the best time of all the year for remembering it. "The Word became flesh and dwelt among us, full of grace and truth." That is Christmas, and Christmas is spoken here. It will always be spoken here.

Lord, You have spoken to us in the birth and life and death of Jesus, and Your Word is plain. Help us to hear it and respond with all our hearts. For there is no other word as intelligible, or important, or loving as this one. Amen.

2

Christmas Is for Simple Folk

A *New Yorker* cartoon showed a business executive—with a grouchy look on his face—standing behind his desk reading a memo from his secretary. "While you were out," it said, "Mongol hordes swept across Asia. Dempsey KO'd Firpo. The cow jumped over the moon. Sherman took Atlanta. Vander Meer pitched a no-hitter. Jazz came up the river."

Have you ever had that feeling—that everything happened while you were out? That history was made while you slept? That the children grew up while you weren't looking? That the most important things in life passed you by because you were not aware of them? Its a real problem, isn't it? Rip van Winkle had nothing on most of us. Life gets to going so fast that before we know it we're gray headed and don't know where the years have gone. Everything seems to be a blur. And worst of all is the feeling that we've missed everything important

—even birthdays and holidays. We just weren't up to them.

How about Christmas? Will you have Christmas this year? Or will it pass you by too?

It is interesting, in the light of the *New Yorker* cartoon, to reflect on the biblical accounts of that first Christmas. Christmas did not come that year to any business executives. In all those reports of dreams and visions—it was a busy angel!—there was not a single "important" person. No emperor received word of the birth of Jesus. No senator knew about it. No financier was let in on it. No famous writer—no media person—got wind of it. Just think, it happened without television! Herod eventually learned of it—but only after the Wise Men visited him. Christmas came in obscurity and anonymity, and most people, that first Christmas, never knew it.

What does this say about Christmas?

Well, for one thing, it says that *Christmas is a gift.* It is not a commodity to be purchased or an occasion to be manipulated. Even the best managers cannot "manage" Christmas into being a success. Not even the churches can bring it off. All our efforts to have Christmas are doomed to failure—unless God gives it to us. Christmas is God's gift to the world, and it can only be received. It cannot be managed.

Do you understand that? Have you ever

knocked yourself out to make Christmas a success—decorating and baking and buying presents and sending cards—only to feel like Scrooge on Christmas Eve and realize that nobody makes Christmas; you either receive it or you don't? We cannot make Christmas—or Easter—happen on command: not with all the tinsel and colored lights and Perry Como music in the world.

Christmas is gift, and the best Christmases have a giftlike quality about them. Isn't that true in your experience? I remember two of the finest Christmases of my life. One we celebrated in Paris when our children were small. We were living on a meager income in a small garret apartment. We set our little tree on a window ledge. Decorations were sparse, and presents were few. But on Christmas Eve we heard a marvelous new cantata by Edmund Pendleton, and then went to midnight mass at Saint Sulpice where Pendleton's master, the great Marcel Dupré, played the organ. Back in the apartment, we kissed the sleeping children and looked out at the twinkling white lights strung in trees along the river Seine. It was all gift.

The other Christmas I recall was two years later. We went to a midnight Communion service at a church in Nashville, Tennessee. Our youngest son, who was five, leaned sleepily against his mother. The other boy, who was eight, watched and listened through the entire service, his wide eyes glowing. As the bread and juice were passed, he whispered to me that he would like to take Communion. I looked at his mother. She looked at me. He was not legally a member of the church. But we knew he understood, and I nodded yes. It was his first time. I am sentimental, and the tears coursed down my cheeks. When we came out, heavy, wet flakes of snow were falling. That Christmas, too, was a gift. We had not planned it at all.

There is another thing about Christmas. *The gift is best known in simplicity and silence.* Think of those to whom the first Christmas was known: an old priest in the Temple; two women of obscurity; a humble carpenter; some shepherds sitting quietly on the hillside; and, later, a handful of Wise Men, watchers of stars and brooders on the night. No complicated people. Only simple folk. Only people with time to feel and reflect and hear heavenly voices.

There again is our problem, isn't it? We are too busy to feel and reflect. Left alone a few minutes, we hear nothing but the beating of our own mad hearts. There is no depth in us where the the voices can find resonance.

Do you remember the line spoken by the simple maid in Shaw's play *Saint Joan* to the colorful figure of the archbishop, standing before her in the brilliant plumage of his office? "What a pity, that though you are an archbishop the voices do not speak to you." What a pity! The world passes us by, and the voices do not speak.

Have you ever sat in some deep silence, perhaps in a church or cemetery or in the woods, in some cathedral of the forest, and felt that you were at the very center of the world? You were. When we are at the center, the voices speak to us, and the visions come. That is when things fall into perspective, and we know their value. Not when we are noisy, rushing about, getting things done. But when we are quiet. When the soul is listening.

"Don't just do something: stand there." That is the real wisdom of life. But we are so busy going and doing and making. It seems to be our nature in the Western world. And we miss so much.

Not everyone reads or agrees with Carlos Castaneda's books, but he tells a good story about the old Yaqui soothsayer named Don Juan. Don Juan doesn't work at anything. He is a wise man, a poet of the soul. Once Carlos asks him what he does in life. Don Juan replies that he is a seer. Carlos says, "I see things too." The old man is quiet for a minute. Then he says, "No, you only think you see, but you don't." "I think I do," says Carlos. "No," says the old man firmly, "you only think you see."

I suspect he was right—that he saw things

Carlos could not see, things most of us cannot see. Because he was quiet and simple. Because he listened. Because he lived in the desert, in the silence.

One of the little ironies of the Gospel of Mark, which from beginning to end makes a great deal of the importance of seeing, occurs in the tenth chapter as Jesus made His way to Jerusalem shortly before the crucifixion. The disciples, blundering souls whom they were, had been doggedly unable to see the true messiahship of Jesus. And then here, as Jesus passed the outskirts of Jericho, a blind man called out, "Jesus, Son of David, have mercy on me!" He saw what the others could not see, and he was blind.

How often it is the blind or the deaf or the handicapped of the world see what the rest of us miss because we are so busy. We make things happen. We cannot receive things.

Christmas is a reminder of the importance of silence and watching. Jesus, if we could imagine His being born today, would not appear in a Hyatt House or in the executive suite of the Time-Life building; He would be born among coal miners in West Virginia or dirt farmers in Mexico or in some remote fishing village of China. And when He comes in His communing presence, as we believe He does, it is to the heart that is able to wait in stillness. The gift is known in simplicity and silence.

Suppose He does come, and you and I have Christmas this year. How shall we respond? There is also a clue to that in our Scriptures. We shall behave as did old Zechariah, Elizabeth and Mary, and the shepherds who came to the manger—*with wonder and adoration*. What did Luke say? That the shepherds told of the angels who had brought them to Christ, and all of them —all those at the manger—were filled with wonder. And the shepherds returned to their fields, "glorifying and praising God for all they had heard and seen" (Luke 2:20).

I expect we shall feel the same way, if we have watched and waited as they did. We shall hear the carols on Christmas Eve, look into the candlelight, taste the bread and wine in our mouths, and become children of faith again. Our hearts will fill with wonder, and we will have a sense of spiritual renewal for our journeys.

I say this because it has happened before. We have waited in simplicity and quietness at other Christmases, and we have experienced the Presence. There is reason to believe, if our hearts are right, that it will happen again. And, when it does, it will be as real and exciting as if it were for the first time—as if it had never happened before.

Paul West, the British writer, had a little daughter who was deaf and retarded. He wrote a marvelously sensitive book about their relationship, called *Words for a Deaf Daughter.* In the book he describes a typical Christmas Day with the girl. She sits, after all the presents have been opened, and clamps her hands over her eyes until one of them, her father or mother, takes one of her presents out of the room and rewraps it. Then, when the present is brought back, she pounces upon it with joy, rending the paper and pulling off the ribbon. She squeals with delight, as if she has never seen the present before—less interested in the thing itself than in the excitement of the process. Again and again the act is repeated. Even when one of her old toys is rewrapped—one from a previous Christmas—there is the same shrieking with joy, as if, says West, it were all some great, exciting mystery she wants repeated over and over.

It is a mystery, isn't it? Christmas itself is a mystery. That is why we want it repeated and repeated. Because our lives are starved for mystery. Because mystery delights us and excites us, the way the packages excited the little girl.

So let's not miss it this year.

Let's not miss it by being too busy, by overdoing, by trying to "manage" its coming.

Instead, let's begin now to take time to prepare our spirits—time to wait in silence—time to pray—time to still the busy wheel of life. And God, who has a way of making worlds out of nothing, will come in our quietness to visit us. That is the gospel, that He does come to us. We can receive Him. We do not have to let the most important thing in the world pass us by.

Lord, teach us the beauty of stillness, of waiting until Your presence forms in our midst. Help us to have the eyes of children for seeing the mystery of Christmas and the miracle of all our relationships in the world, and we shall worship You in wonder and adoration. Through Jesus Christ our Lord. Amen.

3

What Are You Expecting for Christmas?

What are you expecting for Christmas this year? Smoke curling from chimneys into cold skies and bare trees standing like sentinels watching for Santa Claus with his sleigh full of toys? A tall fir tree bedecked with soft colored lights and trinkets and candy canes? The smell of Christmas cookies wafting through the house, and the sound of bells and laughter on the stereo? Children hanging their stockings on the mantle, or, if the stockings have gotten too large and the gifts too plentiful, laying them on the hearth by a blazing fire?

It is easy to think of Christmas images, isn't it, because there is no season of the year so full of nostalgia and ripe with expectation. It takes a Scrooge, with a heart of stone, not to become excited about the approach of this joyous occasion. Visions of sugarplums—or their contemporary equivalent—dance in all our heads.

But I wonder, have you ever been disappointed by Christmas? Did you expect something for Christmas that didn't materialize? Maybe you were looking for a bonus in your pay envelope that wasn't there or expecting somebody home who didn't arrive or anticipating something, a mood or a feeling, that never quite came to you. Maybe you didn't receive a present you were looking for—the doll you had seen in the toy shop or the drum set that would have driven Mom and Dad crazy or the microwave oven you had hinted about for months.

Have you had that experience? I have. I remember once, when I was about six years old, having an absolute passion for an airplane: not a toy airplane but a real one that would fly. I wanted to be able to fly around my neighborhood and look down on all the trees and houses. And I knew Santa Claus was going to bring me an airplane because I had written and asked him for one. My parents tried to warn me, but my faith was unshakable. And I'll never forget my disappointment that Christmas morning when I went into the living room where our tree was and found not an airplane but a puppy.

I have a friend named Dennis Benson who wanted an animal for Christmas. Only he didn't want a puppy, he wanted a kangaroo! He dreamed of that kangaroo the way I dreamed of an airplane. *Wouldn't it be wonderful,* he thought, *to have a pet that could jump over a car!*

And that could fight! Oh boy, he thought, *I could turn my kangaroo loose on anybody who tried to threaten me.* His parents, like mine, tried to dissuade him. But he, like I, couldn't hear. In fact, he took all their hints about what they were getting him as confirmations of his receiving a kangaroo. "This present I am getting," he would say, "would people notice me if I took it to school with me?" "Well, yes," his parents admitted, "they probably would." *Wow,* he thought, *it's a kangaroo!* "Will I have a lot of fun with it?" he asked. "Of course you will," said his parents. *Oh boy,* he thought, *a kangaroo!* The high point of his expectations came on Christmas eve when his parents told him they had to go down to the railway station for something and that he should stay home and not come outside when they returned. He knew it was the kangaroo they were going for. When his parents came home, they drove into the garage, stayed there a few minutes, came out, and shut the doors tightly. Dennis nearly went crazy with excitement. He knew that kangaroo was out there hopping around in the garage. That night, after he went to bed, Dennis heard his father opening the garage doors, and then heard noises as he brought something into the house. Dennis went to sleep imagining he heard the kangaroo bounding around in the living room downstairs. He had never been so excited in his life. The next morning he broke a rule he had never broken: He rushed down to the living room before anybody else was ready to go in. He just had to see that kangaroo before breakfast! Only there wasn't a kangaroo. His mystery present was a big wire recorder—one of the early forerunners of the modern tape recorder. Dennis raced back upstairs and buried his face in his pillow and cried and cried. His parents never knew, he says, how utterly and miserably disappointed he was.

Christmas can be that way. We can build up such impossible hopes and dreams that it can't possibly fulfill them. That is one reason people often feel depressed when Christmas is over. They have lived for days in a state of perpetual excitation, expecting something to happen; and, when it doesn't, they feel sad and let down.

That's too bad because you know what the real message of Christmas is about? It's about what we *don't* expect. That's right. Christmas isn't about what we expect; it's about what we don't expect.

Think about it. Zechariah and Elizabeth didn't expect to have a baby in their old age. Mary didn't expect to become the mother of the Son of God. She couldn't believe it when the angel told her. "Why, I'm not even married," she said. Joseph didn't expect his young bride to be pregnant. Herod didn't expect to be disturbed by word of the Child. The shepherds didn't expect to see angels in their fields. The Magi didn't expect to find the Savior of the world born in a manger in a poor little country village like Bethlehem. The whole thing was a surprise. God surprised everybody that first Christmas.

And when you think about Jesus' teachings, you realize that surprise is in the nature of who God is. God is full of surprises.

The meek shall inherit the earth. Think about that. That's really a surprise, isn't it? When you look around and see the people who shove and push and talk the loudest getting ahead of everybody else, you wonder about the meek.

The first shall be last and the last first. That's another corker. The high and the mighty going into heaven behind the low and the poor. Civic leaders and captains of industry and ministers of big-steeple churches going in behind children and widows and the failed and the jobless.

Full of surprises.

And the resurrection was the biggest surprise of all: Jesus crucified, dead, and buried. His body beaten until His back was like hamburger. His hands nailed to a cross. A spear thrust unceremoniously into His side. His crumpled remains anointed and wrapped and placed in a tomb. A stone rolled across the entrance. Guards posted to turn back trouble. And presto! He came back to life, bigger than life. No magician could ever duplicate the resurrection. It was the greatest surprise of all time.

You see, it isn't a matter of what we're expecting for Christmas. It's what we *don't* expect. That's what we ought to be looking for, what we don't expect because that's the way God is. God is a God of surprises.

I don't have anything against traditional Christmas celebrations. In fact, I love them. I enjoy the trees and lights and Christmas pageants and music and presents and all the rest. But we ought to realize that God may have some surprises in store for us this Christmas. God may not come to us in the old familiar ways. God may speak to us in some new event, in some place where we least expect it.

That's what happened to my friend Dennis Benson. I didn't finish his story. After his disappointment, Dennis began to play around with the wire recorder. Soon he was making up little programs, recording music off the radio and interviewing friends. His interest in recording grew and grew. After he had gone to college and become the youth director of a church, he developed extraordinary programs for young people around music and recorded interviews. When I met him in Kansas City a few years ago, he had become one of the most-celebrated experts on church and media in our country. His books were selling by the thousands, and he was speaking and giving media demonstrations in churches and universities all across the nation. And it all sprang out of the Christmas gift he didn't want, out of the time he was disappointed at Christmas. God surprised Dennis with something he wasn't expecting.

Jesus told the parable of the workers in the vineyard (Matt. 20:1-16) because God continues to surprise us. It's a beautiful little story and full of the gospel. The owner sent a crew of men to work in his vineyard. A few hours later he sent some more. Then, when he paid them, he gave the ones who started late the same as the ones who had started at the beginning of the day. The ones who had worked the longest complained. "Hey!" they said, "this isn't fair." But the owner said, "Whose vineyard is it? I can do what I want." Surprise! God can reward us even when we haven't worked very much. His kingdom is a kingdom of grace, not works. His banquet table is crowded by harlots and publicans. He is a God of surprises, and we can never figure Him out ahead of time.

Robert McAfee Brown, the noted theologian, said the same thing when looking back over his life. Brown wrote a kind of autobiography called *Creative Dislocation: The Movement of Grace.* Creative dislocation: What Brown saw was that the greatest things that had happened to him were things he never expected, things he didn't plan for, things that didn't seem like blessings at the time. "To speak of grace," he said, "is to say that the things most worth expecting are the things that are unexpected." You see, it's the same thing as in the Christmas story and in Dennis Benson's life and in the parable of the workers in the vineyard: Grace is the way God has of surprising us.

So, this Christmas, let's wise up. Let's not look for God in all the familiar places, in the hymns and carols and fireside readings of the Christmas story. Let's look for God in places where we never thought to look—in our failures and burdens and losses; in the cake we *didn't* bake, the person we *didn't* hear from, the guest who didn't come, the job we lost, the course we flunked, the relationship we botched; in the illness that kept us in bed or the party we weren't invited to or the present we didn't receive. Who knows? Maybe, looking back from the perspective of the years, we will think it is the best Christmas we ever had.

May I share with you a story I heard recently from a man in Indiana? He and his family received something unexpected last Christmas: Their home burned on Christmas Eve. It was a large old house they had remodeled themselves. The fire started in some defective wiring. They lost everything except a few picture albums, a small table that had belonged to the man's grandmother, and a few clothes they managed to throw out a window. They spent Christmas Eve in a neighbor's house, shocked and grieved by what had happened. On Christmas they walked through the snow to inspect the charred ruins of the home. They were grateful, the man said, that none of them had been hurt. That afternoon, they began to receive visits and phone calls from people all over the city. Most people who came brought presents: clothes, food, toys for the children, poinsettias, and other things. Two builders who were out of work came and offered their services free to help rebuild the house. "When we went to bed on Christmas Eve," the man said, "we were exhausted and sick at heart. We thought it was the worst Christmas we had ever seen. But by the time it was over, we realized it was probably the best we'd ever had because we learned what wonderful folks our friends and neighbors are." "Would you do it over again?" I asked. "Not by choice," he said. "But looking back on it, it was a warm and beautiful experience."

The surprises of God! We never know where they are or when they are coming. But the word of the gospel is that they are and that they do come. And this is what Christmas is all about.

Your grace, O Lord, is not only sufficient but superabundant, filling our cups to overflowing. Teach us to see it and, having seen, to share it. In the name of Christ. Amen.

4

Everybody Ought to Have a Jewish Mama

I know this title sounds facetious. Actually, it is a quotation—or as near as I can get it by memory—from a statement by novelist Philip Roth. Roth was answering a question about the wonderful, overprotective mother in his novel *Portnoy's Complaint*. The portrait, he said, was drawn largely from real life, from his own mother and other mothers he had known in the Yiddish community. It was a humorous portrait of an old-fashioned mother who hovered over her infant until he was a grown man, reminding him to change his underwear, eat his chicken soup, and wear his scarf in the wintertime. Did Roth mind having such a mother? someone asked. "Everybody," he said with obvious affection, "ought to have a Jewish mama."

I am frankly glad that Christmas always gives us another occasion to remember the Jewish mama of Jesus and, by extension, the other Jewish mamas of the world. I suppose the greeting

39

and... our own!

card people knew what they were doing when they managed to get Mother's Day sequestered into the month of May, which otherwise would be a pretty blah month for greeting card companies. But a good case could be made, I think, for observing Mother's Day in December when we naturally think of Mary. What she has meant to the world through the memory of the church has done much to raise the estate of womanhood from the level it occupied in her day.

Indeed, what Mary has meant to the world has quite altered the way we remember Christmas itself. For, consider, there was very little that was in anyway romantic about that original Christmas. First, there was enemy occupation—the sometimes beneficent but always firm and often galling presence of foreign soldiers throughout the Holy Land. The Jews never took kindly to this, under the best of circumstances. Then there was the requirement that everyone return to his home city to be reregistered for taxation—never a pleasant subject, even under one's own choice of governments. And, to make matters worse, Mary was far into her pregnancy when the trip had to be made. Imagine the weary miles that were traveled, walking the stony roads or bumping along on the spine of a donkey. Not finding an inn to stay in was perhaps no real disappointment, for most stables were probably as comfortable as the inns and houses of the day. But we are not to forget the crudity of birthing in those days, unenhanced as they were by notions of sterility and modern obstetrical aids. It was a dangerous, critical time, especially for a woman far from home and away from female relatives. Finally, there is that part about the massacre of the innocents and the flight into Egypt. Herod, fearing the prophecies of a male child who would be the Messiah, peremptorily ordered all Jewish male children under the age of two years to be slain. And Joseph, being warned of this in a dream, took Mary and Jesus and made the long trek into Egypt until it was safe to return to their home in Nazareth, in the north country.

This is what I mean when I say that Mary has altered the way we remember Christmas. The softness and tenderness of the manger scene, with angels hovering near, overwhelms whatever memory we have of the brutality and agony of the time. The crèche, not the massacre, remains as the symbol of Christmas. The mother and Child provide the focus for our thoughts, not Herod and his bloody troops. Through the long night of the Middle Ages, the madonna and Child commanded the attention of artists and gave us the legacy of mothering and femininity we have never forgotten.

Protestantism, it needs to be said, lost something important in the excesses of its revolt against Catholicism and Mariolatry. It threw out, not the baby with the bathwater, but the mother with mother-worship. In doing so, it cut itself off from the venerable tradition of the Earth-mother, which early Christianity had managed to conscript as one of the great psychic images of the ages. Most ancient cultures knew the figure of the earth-mother.

The one we know best, of course, is classical Greece, with its story of Demeter, whose very name indicated her role as primordial mother. Even as late as the last century, farmers continued to make annual pilgrimages to Eleusis, where celebrations in honor of Demeter took place. I once rode there on a bus and marveled at the distances ancient peoples would walk to get there. At the height of the secret ceremonies, it is said, swine would be slaughtered and an ear of corn raised high in the air, in recognition of the earth goddess who made life fruitful. Christianity incorporated this mythological resource into its adoration of Mary, the virgin mother who brought forth the fruit of God's Spirit, Jesus.

If I may be permitted a moment's digression, this is a part of our understanding of woman that should not be lost in the modern emphasis on the liberation of women. Woman, at her highest, is mother. It is a psychic understanding, a deep-seated intuition, we shall never outgrow. I heard Sister Aquin O'Neill, a professor of literature at Johns Hopkins University, make this observation in a lecture on "The Bible and Southern Womanhood." Scores of women's liberationists in the audience were delighted that a woman was participating in a distinguished lectureship. "You may not like this," she said, "but it is the black mama who is the real heroine in southern literature. Not the Scarlett O'Haras but the Dilseys. Not the proper, beautiful southern belles but the wise and strong mothers of the slaves and sharecroppers. They hold the world together, and women will have lost something if they renounce this mothering role. The world will have lost something too."

I say Protestantism has lost something in purging our religion of Mary except for the Christmas memory. We never escape the need for mother, for the mothering side of God, which Mary helped to secure in Catholicism. Women's liberation is right to accuse Protestantism of a tendency toward maleism, with an exclusively male trinity; we have lost the balance that was preserved in Catholicism. Now we need to feel the motherside, the cradling side, the earth-warming side. We need the caretaking, germinating, hovering figure of the female. Religion becomes one-sided without it. As Goldmund says in Hesse's famous novel, *Narcissus and*

Goldmund, "Without a mother, one cannot die."
We need the Jewish mama.

But what does the Jewish mama have to do
with the kingdom of God? That is what Protestantism asked and why it rejected the mama. It
rejected the mama because she seemed extrane-
ous to the justification theme so central to the
Reformation. It rejected her because she appeared to touch the gospel story only tangential-
ly, not integrally, because the Reformers saw
the gospel primarily in terms of the crucifixion
and resurrection and little else.

Now we must admit that those stark times,
with all their heroism and boldness, missed a
crucial point in the psychological reality of
things. They missed the fact that birth—even
new birth, the birth of the Spirit—is a trauma
that only a mother figure can minimize. This is
the famous discovery and lifelong subject of Otto
Rank, of course, that birth is a trauma, a shock
to the system that we never forget. And if there
is no mama to minimize it, if it doesn't get mini-
mized, if the mama doesn't care, then all life
becomes a trauma to be resisted. The result in
the personality is tension, resistance, fear, and
insecurity throughout life. The personality is
forever marked by the lack of mothering.

Tension, resistance, fear, insecurity are all
traits or qualities of Pharisaism, the name given
to religion that is legalistic, defensive, and

hyper-restrictive. It was the religion that crucified Jesus because He was free and open with
life, because He was not marked by tension, resistance, fear, and insecurity, because He was at
home in the world where Pharisaism was not.

Do you see? Is the picture taking shape? Jesus
was a free man. He strode the earth as if He
belonged here, as if it were good and as if life in
it were to be lived and enjoyed. He showed signs
of mothering. He had been detraumatized. His
birth had in fact become the symbol of God's
incarnation in creation, God's presence in the
earth. The fear process was reversed. Life was
for thanksgiving and celebration, not sadness
and complaints. And Mary—the mother—had
much to do with this. Jesus was a free and open
personality to some extent because of the mother who cradled and loved Him, the mother who
sang praises to God for giving her such a Son,
the mother who remained near Him during His
ministry, the mother who stood by the awful
cross when her Son was executed. The mother,
the mother, the mother—she cannot be written
out of the picture.

Who was it, Camus, who said shortly before
his death that two things remained as the significant factors in his life and writing? One was
the Algerian sunscape—the warmth and brilliance of the sand and the sun and the sea, per-
meating his memory even through the long,

dismal winters of Paris during the war. The other was his mother. His mother was a mute and had never spoken. His father died in World War I when Camus was only a year old. His mother worked as a charwoman to support her family, going out early in the morning and returning late at night. Camus had felt a strange, mystic companionship with her all those years, enhanced by the fact that they always dwelt in silence. Her immutable presence, he said, stood solidly at the center of all he had ever written or accomplished.

Must it not have been the same with Jesus? Why otherwise the tender care in the last desperate hours of the cross, when He commended her into the keeping of the youngest disciple: "Woman, behold thy son!" . . . Behold thy mother!" (John 19:26-27, KJV).

Everybody ought to have a Jewish mama.

The good news of the gospel is, of course, that everybody does. God is like the Jewish mama who cares, overcoming the lack of a natural parent who does. There are no orphans in God's universe, no motherless children. God is love. God is like a mother as well as Father. He manifested Himself in Mary as well as in Jesus, in the women disciples as well as the men disciples. Even though Jewish culture was sexist—there is no mama in the story of the prodigal son—God came through as both male and female. He had his tender, feminine side as well as his strong, masculine side. God disciplines us, but also cradles us. God chastises, but blesses. God rebukes, but loves. God is like the Jewish mama we need.

There is one more thing to say. The nurturing kingdom makes Jewish mamas of us all. To be cared for by God makes us care too. It is a mystery of life. To be loved makes you a lover. To feel the goodness of God makes you want to share it. To be secure causes you to extend security to others. To be received home the way the prodigal was makes you want others to have a homecoming too.

Let me illustrate it this way: I watched a friend, a woman, enter a sharing group. She was tight and nervous at first, easily irritated, and very self-conscious. Her background, it came out, had been one of stress and hardship, of longing for approval but never having it. Gradually, in the group, she learned that she could say whatever she felt without shocking or alienating the others; they were invariably patient and understanding. Over the months of the group's existence, the others convinced her that they actually cared for her—she could be whatever she wished, almost do whatever she wished, without jeopardizing the relationship.

Slowly this understanding transformed her. The energy she had used to maintain her façade was no longer diverted from the joy of living.

Now it all went straight into living. Her behavior was greatly modified. Even her appearance changed. She looked younger and more vital. Her face became illuminated from behind by the new zest she felt for living. But the process did not stop there. In her new radiance, this blossoming woman displayed a strong concern for others who were nervous or ill at ease with life. She became a mothering person, thoughtful and keenly solicitous of others. It was as if this new caretaking self had been imprisoned all those years by the old anxious self and was now released to serve the world.

That is what I mean when I say that the gospel of the kingdom frees us all to become Jewish mamas. When we find life and freedom in Christ, our inner selves are released to minister to others. Caring for the world becomes important to us. Our energies are no longer exhausted in preserving the self. They are allowed to flow uninterruptedly into loving activities for others. Our experience of God as the Jewish mama sets us free to become God's extensions in the world. Suddenly, the words of Jesus strike us with the force of fresh understanding: "A new commandment I give to you, that you love one another; even as I have loved you" (John 13:34). It is the most sensible, inevitable thing in the world! We are loved; therefore, we love.

Then we are caught up in Mary's song and her song becomes our song:

Tell out, my soul, the greatness of the Lord,
rejoice, rejoice, my spirit, in God my Saviour;
so tenderly has he looked upon his servant,
    humble as she is.
For, from this day forth,
all generations will count me blessed,
so wonderfully has he dealt with me,
    the Lord, the Mighty One" (Luke 1:46-50, NEB).

O God, who art our Holy Parent, give us in this time of stress and anxiety a deep sense of Your mothering, that we may in turn become caretakers to one another and to our world. Through Him who was born of Mary. Amen.

5

Are You Giving Any
Christmas Presence This Year?

What are you giving for Christmas this year? There are surely some imaginative things on the market. For example, there is a purse-sized calculator with miniature typewriter keys so the operator can imprint messages to remember what the numbers are for. For lazy telephone dialers, there are telephones with a memory capability of twenty-four preprogrammed numbers, plus automatic redialer for getting those hard-to-reach numbers of talkative friends. For languorous bathers, there are colorful soap caddies with built-in miniature television sets. And for those whose children are slow learners, there are computers that orally drill them in such subjects as math, spelling, and geography. One can hardly help wondering, in the light of such an Aladdin's array of potential gifts, what the baby Jesus would receive if He were being born this year. Would the Magi bring a butane bottle warmer for the manger or a jeweled pedometer for the flight into Egypt? Would there be a dozen thermal diapers or a baby bathtub with built-in water heater and head phones? The Magi were dull and unimaginative gift bringers, weren't they? They only brought gold and frankincense and myrrh. Imagine! These must have been on everybody's gift list that year.

Seriously, present giving has become a problem for many of us, hasn't it? Our lives are so saturated by "things" that the exchange of gifts has become an act of redundancy. Some of us spend half our summer vacations at the beach or in New York or Europe searching for unusual Christmas presents. And then, as Christmas approaches, we check our lists and panic in the realization that we forgot to include Uncle Elmo's third wife or the boss's pet poodle. Christmas gets all but buried beneath our haze of good intentions and the stress of acquiring, wrapping, and delivering packages. One could almost wish the Magi had not brought any presents and started this business of giving things at Christmas!

But let's look at Matthew 2:11 a moment. The Magi brought fabulous gifts to the Christ child. Gold, frankincense, and myrrh were royal presents, the kind brought from one king to another. For the writer of the Gospel, they were a symbol of the extraordinary status of the Child born in lowly circumstances. Yet there is more

to the verse than that. Our imaginations fasten
upon the gifts because they were so opulent. But
the important verb in the passage is not *gave* or
presented (they gave Him gifts) but *prostrated*
(they fell down and worshiped Him). The central
idea of the text is that the Magi, important visitors from the East, came a long distance in order
to prostrate themselves at the feet of the infant
King; and then the Greek word for *gave* or *presented* takes on the additional meaning, which it
has elsewhere in the New Testament, of *offering
up* in royal homage. In other words, the Magi
came to give themselves to Christ. The other
gifts were incidental, mere symbols of their self-
oblation.

There is great truth in this for Christmas.
Christmas is not a time to knock ourselves out
in the ever-increasing task of shopping. Christmas is a time for prostrating ourselves before
Christ, for emptying ourselves before the King
of kings and Lord of lords. The big gift we should
give every year is not a TV set or a video game
or a fur-trimmed negligee; it is our *selves!* Therefore, the tongue-in-cheekiness of this sermon title: it is not a matter of *presents,* spelled
p-r-e-s-e-n-t-s, but of *presence,* spelled *p-r-e-s-
e-n-c-e. We* are the Christmas gifts that matter.

It matters first that we give ourselves to
Christ. While Christmas has many secular con-
nections, it did not begin as a secular holiday. It

began as a festival of the church to remember the coming of God's Son into the world for the salvation of all people. There is something unforgivably rude about conducting our Christmas affairs as if they had nothing to do with the One whose arrival they initially celebrated.

Picture, if you will, a scene in which a very important person comes to visit in the lobby of a great hotel. All the guests in the hotel, apprised of his coming, are in a mood of celebration. They are so jubilant, in fact, that they have all bought gifts to exchange with one another. And, when the important person arrives, they are so caught up in the gift giving that they do not even notice his arrival but celebrate as if he were not even there. That is the way Christmas must appear to Christ if it is not first and foremost a giving of ourselves to Him. Christmas is a time for worship, for rediscovering the dimensions of our faith and commitment to the Lord of all.

Imagine this fancied scene in heaven: Peter says to Jesus, "Lord, why are You looking so glum? Just think, tomorrow is Your birthday! Everybody will be celebrating. There will be cake and Christmas strudel, and all the little angels will sing carols while the candles are lit on the giant tree in the center of Heaven Square." "I know," says Jesus, "it's My birthday that's depressing me." "Oh, surely not," says

Peter. "Why, Lord, You don't look a day older,
though you've been around since the beginning
of time." "It's not that, Peter," says Jesus, "it's
them (pointing to earth), the people down there.
They'll be celebrating too. But most of them
have missed the point entirely. They won't remember that it's My birthday. They'll be so
caught up in their feasting and merrymaking
that they won't think of Me at all. They pray less
on Christmas than almost any other time.
Christmas is one of the loneliest days of the year
for Me."

Let's remember that Christmas is a time for
being present to Christ, for worshiping the One
who was born in Bethlehem. Advent and Christmas begin the Christian year, the start of the
cycle that runs through Lent and Easter and
Pentecost. If we fail to give ourselves to Christ
now, the whole year of faith is thrown off balance.

Now, by the same token, Christmas is a good
time to give our selves to other people—not just
our presents, but our presence. The irony of the
season is that we are often so busy with shopping, wrapping, decorating, and getting ready
for Christmas that we have less time for the
important persons in our lives than at other seasons of the year. We neglect the very people we
are trying to remember.

A few Christmases ago, there was a beautiful

little girl in the hospital at Vanderbilt University. She came from a very wealthy family, and her family showered her with expensive gifts while she was in the hospital. There were great overstuffed toys, including a giraffe that was six feet high, dolls, a dollhouse, and games of every description. The mother, who was well known in social circles, brought something new every time she came to see the little girl. She never stayed long when she came, for she was due at some luncheon or party, but she never failed to bring a gift. The nurses complained about the abundance of toys that made it difficult for them to get about in the room.

One day the little girl was particularly unhappy in the midst of all her fine gifts and held desperately to the mother as the mother sought to extricate herself and not be late to a bazaar. The mother tried to interest the child in the new toy she had brought. "Mommy," cried the little girl, "I want *you!*" Surrounded by gifts, she wanted the most important thing of all, her mother's presence.

I have often thought of that poignant scene at intervening Christmases and hoped that I was not neglecting someone I loved by trying to substitute things for my self. There is nothing any of us has to give that is as rich and fine as the most basic gift of all: the love and devotion of our hearts.

It may be with our children, who are too divorced from the lives and activities of parents these days. It may be with our fathers and mothers, who loved us and had to give us up when we went away and established homes of our own. It may be with friends and associates, who have been let into our lives only part way, without any thought of allowing them more. It may be with our wives and husbands, who are often the most taken-for-granted persons in our lives. It may be with people in prisons of one kind or another, places of confinement because of misdeeds or certain kinds of jobs or ill health. There are many persons with whom we can share ourselves this Christmas and have a richer, more wonderful Christmas than if we owned a department store and could wrap it all up and have it delivered to their addresses on Christmas Eve. The simple gift of the self—of one's undivided time and presence—is the finest thing we have to give.

Think about all the people who are shut-ins at Christmas: the elderly, the hospitalized, and the frail. How much a visit would mean to them! Once in London I ran across a book by Mrs. Leslie Stephens called *Notes from Sick Rooms*. It was an old book about the nursing profession, with helpful hints for persons who were charged with caring for the ill. One suggestion Mrs. Stephens gave was that the nurse might erect a mirror in the room, placed at an angle so the patient could see outside the window. It will, she said, be "a refreshment to the eyes which have for long not pierced beyond the narrow boundary of the sick room." Our visits are such mirrors; they permit people to see outside their rooms, to hear the sounds of busy streets and smell the fresh air through which we have come to their sides. Our presence, in such cases, is much more meaningful than mere presents.

What it comes down to, you see, is incarnation. That is what Christmas is about. Spirit becoming flesh, taking on an earthly presence. God with us: not sending us gifts but with us. And the way we worship God at Christmas or any other time is with our presence, our being, our truest selves. We worship God by caring about Christ and by caring about others in our world. We do not do it by busyness; we do it by being there as fully as we can.

One Christmas story in the Bible rarely gets treated as a Christmas story: It is the story of Jesus in the home of Mary and Martha. You remember it. The two sisters had much to do. They were late with their Christmas preparations. The tree was only half decorated, the gifts were unwrapped, the Christmas pudding had just been plopped into the oven. Martha was scurrying about, trying to get her cards mailed and the mistletoe hung and the cookie dough cut into Christmasy shapes. Mary had a lot to do too; after all, she and Martha lived together, and what one had to do the other needed to get done as well. But Mary took the time to be with Jesus —to sit at His feet and worship Him. And when Martha came to the door with flour on her nose, chiding Mary for not helping, Jesus said, "Martha, Martha, I know you have a lot to worry and fret about, and so does Mary. But Mary has chosen to do the one thing that is necessary, and that is to share her presence with me. She has made the wise choice."

God help us all to be wise this Christmas! Are you giving any Christmas presence this year?

"Dear Lord and Father of mankind,
Forgive our foolish ways;
Reclothe us in our rightful mind;
In purer lives thy service find,
In deeper rev'rence, praise.

"Drop thy still dews of quietness,
Till all our strivings cease;
Take from our souls the strain and stress,
And let our ordered lives confess
The beauty of thy peace." Amen.

6

Christmas Ho-Hum
or Christmas Golly-Gee?

It had not been an easy year for the man of the house. His business was not doing well, and already several employees had been laid off. He was not immediately threatened, but he had begun to ponder the future. His parents had been in a car wreck, and, though they were recuperating nicely, this had caused him some concern. To top it all off, he had turned forty in October and was beginning to confront the fact of his own mortality. His family had noted a sense of gathering gloom in his personality and were wondering what kind of Christmas it would be. His teenage daughter broke the ice. "OK, Dad," she asked, "what's it going to be this year, Christmas ho-hum or Christmas golly-gee?"

Christmas ho-hum or Christmas golly-gee. Which is it going to be for you?

It is easy to fall in the pattern of Christmas ho-hum, isn't it? It seems to happen to most of

us sooner or later. There are good reasons *not* to
be excited about the approach of Christmas.

One reason is that we don't believe it anymore. Oh, we're not out-and-out atheists or anything like that. We just don't feel particularly
moved by the central tenets of our faith anymore. It's as simple as that.

You know what I mean, don't you? A woman
came to see me several months ago. She said, "I
don't know whether I ought to be troubled about
this or not, but I've become aware of a great
apathy in my life for the religious side of my
existence." She couldn't understand it, she said,
because she was raised by God-fearing Metho-
dist parents and had always been an avid church
attender. Then one night she was watching a TV
program about a futuristic world in which a
totalitarian government had suppressed all religious expression—there were no churches or
worship services—and she caught herself saying, "That wouldn't be so bad." This had made
her think about her faith, and she was wondering whether any of it really mattered in her life.

The woman's case was probably not abnormal. We all go through times of inactive faith
when our passion for belief and religious commitment is almost frightening by its absence.
And if we happen to be in one of those times
right now, we're probably going into Christmas
with a very ho-hum attitude.

Another reason for feeling ho-hum about Christmas may be that it is coming at a time when we are tired and distracted. Our faith hasn't exactly waned, but our lives are so full of constant demands at home, at school, in the office, at church, that we simply don't have the energy to cope with the extra demands imposed by the Christmas season. There isn't time in our schedules for parties, shopping, decorating, baking, and all the other things that go with Christmas. We feel like the poor grade-school teacher in the cartoon, who is just seeing the last little darling and his mother out of the classroom after the big Christmas party. "Have a great Christmas!" they are saying to the teacher. The poor creature's eyes are glazed, her hair is messed, her blouse is out, her hose are sagging, and she looks ready to faint dead away.

It is not easy to feel golly-gee about Christmas when one goes into it as a candidate for nervous exhaustion. When we are in that state, Christmas may represent the last straw, the final burden of the year, one more obstacle to be cleared before there's an opportunity to rest and recover strength.

This year, there is another reason many may feel ho-hum about Christmas: They can't afford it. Some people are out of work. Others are on fixed incomes that have not kept pace with inflation. And Christmas, for some families, has become staggeringly expensive.

"Would you believe," said a man to me the other day, "that I am just now making the final payments on last year's Christmas presents? Why, I join a Christmas Club every year in order to be able to cover the interest on next year's gifts!"

It has gotten out of control, hasn't it? Microwaves and lounge chairs and pool tables and dolls with hair that grows and racing bikes and computer consoles and fur coats and sports cars. What happened to the old-fashioned Christmas with oranges and apples and candy sticks and maybe a homemade sweater or a tie and a pair of socks? Maybe we've been sucked in by Madison Avenue. Maybe we've been trying to have an "eschatological" Christmas, the last big one before the bomb falls or the bubble bursts. Maybe we've been on the escalator of giving, with every Christmas getting bigger and richer than the one before and didn't know how to get off.

But you're right if it's your reason for not feeling truly excited about the approach of the jingle-bells season. Most of us can't afford it. Santa Claus isn't a tycoon in a red suit and a long white beard. He's a nine-to-five worker with first-of-the-month problems, and instead of feeling excited he's saying, "Oh no, it's Christmas again!"

Well, I don't want to have a ho-hum Christmas, do you? Isn't Christmas supposed to be full of wonder and joy? What about the good news the angels brought to the shepherds? Should they have said, "We've got good news and bad news"? We seem to know the bad news better than the good. That's our trouble. What is the good news for each of these problems we've talked about?

Let's consider the shepherds a moment. Did it ever occur to you that they may have had as many reasons as we do to feel ho-hum about Christmas? Take the problem of not believing anymore. Do you think they were great believers? Not likely. They were simple sheepherders, not theologians. About religion, they only knew what they heard on the street corner and experienced in the marketplace. They were Jews in a country overrun by Romans—Roman soldiers, Roman tax collectors, Roman tourists, Roman landholders. Why, the very land where they tended sheep was probably owned by some Roman senator basking in luxury on the Isle of Capri. What would they have thought about the ancient promises of God to make Israel into the first nation of the world? That dream must have died a long time ago. They weren't religious men and probably had few religious feelings.

That is what makes the Gospel story so surprising. The angels didn't go to a school of prophets singing hymns in some ancient monastery. They didn't appear to an enclave of priests in the Temple. They went to simple, apathetic shepherds on the hillside and announced, "To you is born this day in the city of David a Savior, who is Christ the Lord." And the shepherds' lives, which had been so empty, were filled with wonder.

We are tired and see Christmas coming toward us as another burden to be borne. They were tired too. We probably don't think of that, but they were. We picture their lives as serene, carefree, and peaceful: no schedules to meet, no traffic to fight, no parties to attend. Simple, unadorned country living. But have you ever tried to herd sheep? Have you ever tried to herd *anything:* goats, cows, chickens, or small children?

I remember when one of our sons first got a job as a lifeguard at a swimming pool. "It'll be a snap," he said, "sitting there getting a tan, relaxing, and watching all the girls go by." He came home at seven, ate a few bites of supper, and fell asleep at eight. "It wears you out," he said, "trying to keep up with all those little children all day. 'Stop that running! Don't carry drinks around the pool! You mustn't fight in the water!' Why, it's the hardest job I've ever had!"

Think about the shepherds, keeping up with

the little lambs and sheep all day long. Is anything dumber than a sheep? And when the shepherds went to bed at night, when they finally got comfortable in their warm bedrolls, I don't imagine they were in any mood to be awakened by heavenly carolers and sent walking into town to see what had come to pass. "That's miles away," one might have said. "I've been on my feet all day."

But the good news must have energized them because they went, and saw, and worshiped. And what they beheld probably energized them the next day, though they had gone without sleep, and for days to come as well. Wouldn't it energize us too if we really perceived Christmas as good news? It might be just what we need to carry us through the season.

And as for not being able to afford Christmas, where do you suppose those poor shepherds stood? Imagine being called into the presence of Christ and wanting to make a gift to Him and and not having anything to give. There is no record that they offered the baby any presents. Maybe they didn't. Or maybe anything they might have given was so overshadowed by the gifts of the wealthy Magi that nobody bothered to remember what they gave.

I can imagine that one of them took the warm, fleecy sheepskin off his shoulders and offered it to Mary for her Child. Maybe one of them carried some cheese made from the milk of a goat that ran with his flock and offered that. Do you remember *The Second Shepherd's Play,* the little Christmas play surviving from the Middle Ages? It is a humorous drama, with some delightful horseplay in it. In the final scene of the play, the shepherds bring their simple gifts to the Christ child. One brings a sprig of cherries. Another brings a bird. And another brings a ball.

The shepherds were poor and hadn't much to give. But when did Christmas ever cost anything to be rich and meaningful? Some of the best Christmases any of us ever had were our poorest, when we made our own decorations and ate simple foods and exchanged homemade gifts. Maybe it is time to restore such Christmases to their place in our lives, if we are out of funds or have merely grown weary of overindulgence as a symbol of grace.

The point is that the shepherds weren't very different from us. They weren't ready for Christmas either. It burst upon them with the light of a thousand suns and exploded in their hearts, like the melody of an angel choir. Their ho-hum became golly-gee, and the whole world looked different to them.

How about you? What kind of Christmas will you have this year? Will it be Christmas ho-hum or Christmas golly-gee?

Fill our hearts with wonder, O God, and make our lives to shine with love again. Let the song of the angels, that changed the shepherds' existence, resound in our ears once more. Through Jesus Christ, the Lord of Bethlehem. Amen.

7

Learning Not to Be Afraid

Recently I read H. A. Williams's autobiography *Someday I'll Find You*. In this treasure chest of a book, Williams, who is one of the leading religious thinkers and preachers of the Church of England, speaks openly of a period of his life when he was totally incapacitated by phobic anxieties. He was afraid to go into the streets or marketplaces. When friends chided him for wearing a pair of shoes that were worn out and falling apart, he did not tell them it was because he was terrified of going into a store to buy more. He could not bear to ride on buses or trains, and subways were completely out of the question. The thought of getting on an escalator or into an elevator filled him with horror. Eventually he was afraid even to leave his room at the university. He became so overcome with anxiety that he was partially paralyzed and could not drag himself across the room. It took years of psychoanalysis to conquer this sense of dread and fear so that he could lead a normal life again.

I thought as I was reading about this of my friend John Denny Newman, whom I had known from childhood and who for a few weeks was my roommate in college. John Denny too was paralyzed by fear. He was too nervous ever to have a date. When he took his college exams his last year in high school, he panicked and broke his glasses in two so that he could not see to complete the exam. He came to college with a large boxful of medicines and ointments, afraid to be so far from his doctor. He was a brilliant boy, but he could not face life. I believe he committed suicide, though his family would never say. He died in his apartment while he was in medical school. He had been dead for several days when his body was discovered. Perhaps he was frightened to death.

Do we have enough respect, I wonder, for the fears of the people around us? For the fear of the child who cannot sleep without a light in the room? Of the woman who cannot stand snakes or the man who is deathly afraid of dogs? Of the mother who knows something is going to happen to her children or the man who always expects to lose his job? Of the student who is convinced he will fail or the surgeon who fears she will make a botch of the surgery and kill a patient? Of the person who is terrified of medica-

tion and the one who cannot face life without it?
Of the church member who sits close to the aisle
at the back in order to get out fast if he or she
becomes panicky or afraid?

The world is full of fears, and most of us, if we
will reflect honestly on our lives, can remember
a time when we were truly afraid. I can remember such moments myself. We all can, if we
think back openly. We have all had our times of
fear and terror.

Had John, the writer of the Epistles, had
them? Is that what he was thinking about when
he wrote, "There is no fear in love, but perfect
love casts out fear" (1 John 4:18)? What had he
been afraid of? Of leaving his parents when
Jesus came by the boat and called him to disci-
pleship? Of the crowds that were always gathered around Jesus? Of the conflict with the
Pharisees who were forever trying to entrap
Jesus with their arrogance, cleverness, and
snide remarks? Of the soldiers in Jerusalem,
who took his Lord away that night in the garden
and crucified him the next day? How did John
feel after that? Did he awaken every night in the
midst of a terrible nightmare, perspiring and
horrified by what was about to happen to him?
Did it take years to get over it? What about the
soldiers who suddenly appeared at Christian
gatherings, slashing about with their swords

and clapping people into prison? Was he afraid of them?

Whatever it was, he had the secret, didn't he? "There is no fear in love, but perfect love casts out fear." The Greek words are emphatic. Perfect love throws fear out, takes it by the scruff of the neck and pitches it into the street, ejects it bodily.

Think about it. It does, doesn't it? Remember the stories you have read about faithful dogs who, when their masters were being attacked by wild animals, would fight to the death to protect them with no thought for their own survival. Imagine the mothers who have raced into burning buildings to rescue their children with no fear of the consequences. A man I know who was shot near the heart by two men staggered for blocks to get help for his family, unmindful of his own fate. Love does throw out all fear, doesn't it?

Even in lesser instances, it works. When I began courting my wife, I was afraid of her father. I weighed about 150 pounds at the time, and he was a big, strapping man of over 200 pounds. He didn't like to have his daughter courted, and he often spoke gruffly or unpleasantly to me. Sometimes he would raise his fist and tell me never to come back to his house. But I loved his daughter so much that I ignored his threats. I won't say that my love cast out all my fear, but it at least mitigated it.

"Perfect love casts out fear."

But what if we don't love enough? What if we can't? What if we try to be loving—think loving thoughts all day, try to remember how wonderful life is, and say over and over to ourselves, "I love, I love, I love"—and still it isn't enough, we still feel afraid?

That's where the gospel comes in. That's the good news the New Testament is about. We don't have to do the loving. God does it! We don't have to generate it on our own. We don't have to read Leo Buscaglia and attend seminars in loving and practice loving every day. God does it! "God so loved the world that he gave his only Son." That's what excited all those early Christian preachers and missionaries. God had expressed His love for the world. "Greater love hath no man than this, that a man lay down his life for his friends." And Jesus did! When we see this—really see it—how can we be afraid? God in love with us. What more can we ask? Doesn't it begin to work on our fear?

This is what the song of the angels was about that first Christmas. "Don't be afraid, we bring you good news, for unto you is born this day in the city of David a Savior!" God's love was manifested in Jesus. We don't have to be afraid anymore.

Is this foolishness? Is it "pie in the sky," an insult to modern intelligence? Or is it the greatest reality and we just haven't tried it, haven't really permitted it to work in our lives?

There will be no convincing you if you want to argue about it. But maybe you will think about it and realize what God has done. "If God is for us," asked the apostle Paul, "who can be against us?" If God loves us, what do we have to be afraid of?

Harry Williams gradually came through his dark times and saw the truth of God's love and ceased to be afraid. It took a long time—several years, in fact—and the love of a good psychiatrist and some faithful friends. But it eventually happened. And, when it did, Harry began to see the whole world as an arena of love, not fear.

Let me give you a "before" and an "after."

Before, when Harry was first coming down with his sickness, he was walking one winter's day in Regent's Park in London. There had been a snow. The air was still, and everything was sublimely beautiful. The shrubs were bursting through their coating of snow as if playing a game. The sun was setting and cast a glow of gold and red over everything. It was both gentle and overpowering, said Harry, and filled with blessedness and love. Or it should have been. For Harry, it wasn't. Instead, it aroused in him a sharp sense of anguish and despair. He wanted to enter the glory that lay around him and become part of it. But he couldn't. He was painfully aware of the difference between him and the park. It was a part of God's world he couldn't truly enter, even though he stood in the midst of it. He felt a thousand times more isolated than he had when he began his walk.

But after his cure—after he had learned to love—it was different. One day Harry went into the cafeteria at Waterloo station. It was crowded with people. He looked at the people, and it came to him with the force of a revelation that he was in the room at Emmaus with Christ and the two disciples who had walked the road with Him. The tea and cakes being consumed by the crowd were the blood and the body of Christ in the Sacrament, and they were all gathered together in the presence of the Lord. It was a beautiful, beatific moment. This time he was not separated from his environment as he had been that day in the park. He was a part of everything. He felt no fear. Perfect love had cast it out.

That's the beauty of the angels' message. We don't have to be afraid anymore. Unto us a Son is born, a Savior is given. And His name is the Love of God.

Surround us with Your love, O God, until all our fears are forgotten and we are joined to all Your saints, both living and dead, forever and ever. Amen.

8

A Gift that Matters

They have called the originators of the BMW syndrome—for Balthazar, Melchior, and that other Wise Man, whatever his name was. There should be plaques to their honor in Neimas-Marcus, Saks Fifth Avenue, Bullocks, and perhaps even in such déclassé merchansiders as Sears, Montgomery Ward, and J. C. Penney. They began the tradition of Christmas giving at such a high level, with gold, frankincense, and myrrh.

Everyone knows what gold is, but perhaps not everybody is so sure about frankincense and myrrh. They were really very similar, one being a resinous, aromatic gum extracted from Oriental balsam trees and the other a resinous, aromatic gum extracted from certain low-growing bushes in Asia and the Middle East. It was a little like giving two fragrances of perfume or two kinds of after-shave lotion. Only, like gold itself, they were both very costly. And one may

have been more associated with royalty and the
other with the anointment of the dead, so that
a cryptic foretelling of Christ's future was involved. But the primary emphasis appears to
have been upon the great value of the gifts. Here
were three or more Oriental astrologists—gurus
or Wise Men—coming to lay their symbols of
wealth and devotion at the feet of the newborn
Savior of the world, and today we can only guess
at the enormous worth of what they gave. Certainly they were no pikers.

I don't know about you, but I have sometimes
wondered what happened to the gold, frankincense, and myrrh. There are no further refer-
ences to them in the Gospels, and Jesus, in His
adult life at least, appears to have been a mendi-
cant, a poor, itinerant teacher who derived His
food and lodging wherever He could. Were the
valuable gifts of the Magi used to finance the
flight into Egypt, which Mary and Joseph under-
took to escape from the evil King Herod? Did
Joseph buy a carpentry shop with them when
the family returned to Nazareth? Or, like a lot
of other expensive gifts, did they end up hidden
in a closet to be divided among the next of kin
when the family passed on? A child, at any rate
—even a holy Child—could hardly have become
excited about gold, frankincense, and myrrh.

In the light of such ponderings, I suppose, I
was delighted with a painting by Sir Anthony

Vandyke I saw a few months ago in the Cour-
tauld Gallery in London. It was called *The Adoration of the Shepherds* and showed the
shepherds of the infancy narratives gathered
around the baby Jesus at the stable, all strain-
ing forward in the magical light to see the Infant
cradled in the straw. And the shepherds' *wives*
were with them—a touch which I thought was
marvelously human! And one of the women was
stretching out her hand to offer the holy Child
an *egg*!

Imagine! An egg for the Baby! What could be
more beautiful? Or more immediately useful—
at least for the parents—in a world where one
didn't run out to the nearest convenience store
for breakfast supplies? It was, as the artist con-
ceived it, one of the loveliest, most graceful ob-
jects in the world. It was richer, in its simple
beauty, than any gem or work of art. An egg for
the Baby!

I thought about that egg recently as I strolled
through a shopping mall among the harried
shoppers getting ready for Christmas. How cluttered our stores are with impractical, unusable
merchandise—oversized stuffed animals; ridiculous furniture and room decorations; gaudy jewelry; silly, superfluous items of clothing; row
upon row of ill-designed, useless pottery and
gewgaws; and electrical gadgets designed to
malfunction the second time they are used. It's

as if everybody in the world already had all the basic, important things and now the entire corporate world is devoted to the production and sale of junk.

Some people are beginning to fight back. One family has decreed that no member is to buy anything for Christmas, that all gifts must be treasured items that will be merely passed around. Another family has said that all gifts exchanged this year must be homemade—nothing from the shopping malls. And yet another family has decided that no gift may cost more than ten dollars; family members are forced back upon their ingenuity to find something of charm and usefulness for very little outlay.

I'm not sure how I feel about this. In our economy, a lot of people depend on a good year of sales in the stores—clerks as well as managers and owners. And I'm not sure that something I made myself wouldn't be more grotesque and useless than some of the things I've described in the stores.

But I have a suggestion about gift giving this Christmas—a suggestion that might help us to relocate Christmas where it ought to be, to set it in a perspective that is at once more human and more gracious and more spiritual. I suggest that we all resolve this Christmas to give some gifts that really matter, gifts that translate immediately into meaning and usefulness for their recipients. And what I have in mind is gifts that don't necessarily cost anything except in terms of thoughtfulness and time and perhaps a little energy. They won't prevent our giving other gifts as well—the traditional ties and socks and jewelry and microwaves—but they will greatly enrich our Christmas season.

For example, what is the most important thing any of us have? It's *time*, isn't it? Time to work, time to play, time to reflect, time to read, time to be. Time is a precious commodity. And, for that reason, what better gift can we give some persons on our list than some of our time? Here is a father who never has time to visit with his children because he is always so busy. What if he took off an entire afternoon while the children are out of school and said, "Look, Mary and Bill, we haven't been to the movies in ages. What do you say we go this afternoon? We'll get some popcorn, and then after the movie we'll go to the ice cream shop for sundaes." Why, that's a gift they would never forget, isn't it? Suppose you took the time to visit a friend you haven't seen in months or to write a long letter to someone who needs to hear from you. Wouldn't that be a gift worth treasuring?

I was so impressed by a letter Karl Menninger, the famous psychiatrist, wrote to a young friend who was dying. Dr. Karl, who was then eighty-three, wrote:

In putting down these words, just as they come to me, word after word—like foot steps—I am coming toward you. I am walking over to put my arms around you and hug you. . . . I'm half a thousand miles away, actually—or at least my body is—and I've lost confidence in my powers of locomotion. But I can fly through the air faster than any airplane in my imagination and thinking, and now I am right there with you— in the room with you. (Letter excerpted in *Wall Street Journal*, Dec. 23, 1985).

He could not go to be with the young friend, but he could take time to write. And we can imagine how thrilled the friend was to receive such a tender, loving letter. I suspect we all have friends who would welcome such a letter from us if we would only make a gift of the time to write.

Then there is the gift of *encouragement* we could give to others. Often it takes very little time to give such a gift, but it means so much. Think of the people who have encouraged you at strategic moments in your life, perhaps by a kind word or a hug or an assurance of their love. Couldn't you do as much for someone this week? Couldn't you go through the Christmas season scattering gifts of this kind?

I think of the evening we were eating in the New London Inn, a pub restaurant in Ashburton, in Devonshire, England. We noticed that the waitress was being exceptionally kind to an elderly couple at another table. Afterwards, when the couple had paid their bill and left, we were talking with her. She told us that the woman had cancer and would soon be gone. "She comes in," said the waitress, "almost every night. I can see her failing every time. But I always say, 'You're looking great,' or 'My, aren't we pretty tonight?' It seems to cheer them up." This woman knew the power of encouragement, and she gave it freely. You can't put a price on a gift like that.

There is also the gift of *prayer*. If we really believe in the power of prayer, wouldn't the Christmas season be a wonderful time to set aside some hours to pray for certain people we know? They don't even have to know we're doing it, unless we can let them know without appearing pious or condescending.

I met a woman named Terry in Anderson, Indiana, a few years ago. She had read my book *Bread for the Wilderness, Wine for the Journey,* which was on the subject of prayer. At a funeral service for a young man who had been killed in a traffic accident, she was sitting behind the mother of the boy whose car had caused the accident. The woman was sobbing so violently that her shoulders were shaking. "I remembered what you said about praying," Terry said, "and I just sort of beamed a little prayer at the woman, trying to support her in a spiritual way." After the funeral, said Terry, she was waiting for a friend and saw this mother coming toward her. She later realized the mother was going toward her car, but at the time she supposed she was coming toward her, and she held out her arms to her. The mother entered the embrace and began sobbing. Terry comforted her and assured her that people understood and didn't blame her son; such things merely happen. The mother finally stopped crying and got into her car. Then she got out again and came back to thank Terry. "It means so much to hear that from a stranger," she said. "Others tell me, but they're friends."

Terry got involved in the mother's life because she prayed for her. The prayer was a gift. The relationship was a gift. What better gift could she have given that mother at the time?

Sometimes we can even go beyond praying for others and give them the gift of *actual help*. That is, there are times when it is in our power to do something for another person that perhaps no one else could do or is willing to do. We can help the person to find a job or get into college or locate a new home or secure a loan or understand the nature of a problem the person is having, and the help is a wonderful gift.

A friend of ours who likes to help people spent a Sunday afternoon making a strawberry pie. "What are you doing that for?" asked her husband. She is a very religious woman. "The Lord will give us somebody to help eat it," she said. When the pie was in the oven, she telephoned some friends to come over and share the pie. But they were all busy and could not come, so the pie went uneaten. That evening she and her husband went to church. After the service she saw a woman standing alone who had joined the church the Sunday before. *She looks lonely*, she thought. So she went up and invited her home to share the strawberry pie. And before she was through, she gathered up several friends to go along. As they were enjoying the pie and sitting around talking, the woman suddenly burst into tears. Our friend went over and hugged her. The woman said, "I'm so happy. I prayed all day that God would would give me some new friends, and here you are." Her husband, it turned out, had deserted her and four small children. Her life had been hard, and she felt bereft and lonely. The whole group became close friends from that night on. "It was the Lord's strawberry pie!" said our friend.

You have the picture don't you? There are many gifts we can give during this Advent season that cost very little or nothing at all, yet matter enormously to those who receive them. We can give books we've read or ideas we've had. We can give our forgiveness to those who need it. Imagine that: calling up someone who has done you harm and saying, "I want to give you a Christmas present; I want you to know I forgive you for what you did." Wouldn't that be something? Or you can give your love and joy to someone—a simple gift—a contagious gift—something to lift someone's spirits and really make Christmas happen.

I have a former student who does this for me. He calls me occasionally just to say hello and to wish me a good day. He doesn't want anything. He makes no demands or requests. He only calls and chats and sends a radiant spirit across the wires. I always feel as if my very skin is smiling after I've had a conversation with him. I hope I hear from him this Christmas. If I don't I will call him, and see if it doesn't work in the other direction too.

That's the point, of course. When we give these gifts that don't cost any money, these gifts of time and encouragement and prayer and help and forgiveness and love and joy, we are enriched as much as those who receive the gifts. They're like boomerangs that come back to us. They give us a sense of what Christmas is all about, of what God meant in sending His Son to be born in a stable.

I knew a man who got involved in the Big Brother movement. He didn't have any children of his own and thought it would be neat to have a relationship with an underprivileged boy, so

he joined Big Brothers. He thought he would
give some boy something special. What he didn't
count on was that he would get something. He
could get tears in his eyes just telling me about
what he experienced with the boys he was big
brother to over the years. It changed his life.

That's what giving like this does; it changes
your life. And, in the end, you're giving something to Christ. You're giving back to Him what
He has given to the world.

We had a lovely director of Christian education at our church in Virginia. Her name was
Betty Jo Kendall. When Betty Jo came to our
church, she organized a children's Christmas
pageant. And she let the children decide on
what gifts they would give the baby Jesus in the
pageant. Some wanted to give Him stuffed animals. Others wanted to give Him toys. One
beautiful little girl name Sallie Baldwin had
several conversations with Betty Jo before she
admitted what she wanted to give the baby
Jesus. Finally Betty Jo asked, "Sallie, what do
you want to give Jesus?"

"Oh, I'm so embarrassed," said Sallie, "I
shouldn't tell you."

"What is it?" asked Betty Jo.

"A kiss," she said.

And, the night of the pageant, that is what she
gave Him. All the other angels brought their

gifts of toys and animals. But Sallie bent over the manger and gave the little baby a kiss.

A loving sigh went up from the congregation as we watched. She knew the secret of giving. The important thing at Christmas is to give something that matters—something from the heart—because the heart is what Christmas is all about.

Enable me to give myself to you, O God, until I am able to give myself to others. Amen.

9

For People Who Have Everything

It is a commentary on our situation in life that the biggest problem most of us have with our Christmas shopping, aside from finding time to do it, is that most of the people we shop for already have everything they need. "I don't know what in the world to get my father this year," said one woman. "Last year I bought him a pearl-handled back scratcher, and the year before that it was a gold-plated cherry pitter. This year I'm fresh out of ideas."

We can imagine the scene in a fairly average household on Christmas morning. When all the expensively wrapped gifts have been opened and the room looks like an explosion in a paper-goods factory, the following inventory is taken: Father received two bathrobes, six shirts, eight ties, four pairs of socks, including a pair of argyles for the golf course, a miniature TV set for use in the bathroom, a car vacuum that plugs into the lighter socket, a bowling ball, and a set of knitted booties for his golf clubs.

Mother acquired a peignoir set, three slips, six pairs of pantyhose in hues of pink and blue, four bottles of perfume and cologne, a microwave oven, an automatic popcorn popper (from Junior, who loves popcorn), a folding hair dryer, and the latest complicated sewing machine, which she will never learn to use.

Junior racked up a computer, six electronic games, an oversized tennis racket, two running outfits, seven recordings, three shirts, a Harris Tweed jacket, two books—which he will never read, a portable electric typewriter, a Bible (from Suzie, who thought he ought to read it), and a high-powered dirt bike.

Suzie came off with a robe, three sets of pajamas, a fur-trimmed coat, portable electric hair curlers, a color TV set, a copy of *Jack the Ripper* (from Junior, who thought she ought to read it), a diamond pendant, a new set of skis, and a round-trip plane ticket to New York City, so she can visit with friends after the holidays.

It is rather obvious, in short, that this typical American family has everything. They have helped keep the economy on an upward spiral, gratifying both the local merchants and the administration in Washington, and they have cluttered their household with many more things that are destined for the school auction or the garage sale when they move or find that their home is simply too overladen for living. They could not possibly want for anything they don't have.

But let's look at them again, more closely this time. Dad's hair is getting thin, and the worry lines on his face are getting thicker. His promotion to vice-president of his company has not come as an unmixed blessing. He has had so little time with his family lately that now, on Christmas morning, he feels like a stranger in his own home. He is out of touch with his own feelings. Several times, during the pre-Christmas season, he felt twinges of nostalgia and almost managed to get ahold of scenes and images out of his childhood memory bag; but each time his energies and schedule were so preempted by other things that he had to let them go before he actually reexperienced them. He has been very much aware of mortality since his predecessor in the vice-president's office had a sudden heart attack, but some days he is so tired of the rat race that the idea of his dying presents itself with more attraction than repulsion.

Mom, too, is growing older and seems to be at a very nervous stage of her life's journey. She couldn't wait till the packages were opened to light up a cigarette. In fact, she's already had three this morning. And now she's opening the liquor cabinet to pour herself a steadier. She belongs to two spas, a diet club, and an exercise group, but she is twenty pounds overweight and takes enough pills of various kinds to fill several beanbags every week. Her hand shakes, her voice quavers, and she cries a lot, often for no good reason. She frequently shouts at the children, curses herself, and locks herself in the bathroom to be alone with her problems.

Even the children have their troubles. Junior is into drugs and has twice in the past year been so sick on beer than he threw up all over himself. He's barely hanging onto a *D* in math and has already thrown in the towel in chemistry, so he will probably have to go to summer school. He worries about the pimples on his face and feels betrayed by friends whenever they forget to invite him to a party. At sixteen Junior wonders how he could mess up his life any worse than he has.

Suzie is only fourteen, but she's already experimenting with heavy sex and smoking an occasional joint. She wanted to be a cheerleader but is too unpopular with the kids to get elected. She curses like a sailor to show everybody she's a hip young woman and makes obscene signs at the teacher when the teacher's back is turned. Already she's running too fast to know who she is and never slows down to look back.

Are they people who *have* everything or people who *need* everything? What do they really need this Christmas?

They need *simplicity*, time for sorting out their lives, time for being together, time for getting to know one another, and time for sharing themselves at the deepest levels of human communication.

They need *holy time*, a sense of life's deeper dimensions, of eternal mysteries breaking in upon finite existence, of the God of righteousness whose being conveys meaning to all of life's actions and relationships, and the blessing of a world that wants to bless us if we'll only let it.

They need *space for seeing life as it is*, for seeing the millions of people in the world who are starving to death and the millions who are dying of simple diseases, for realizing how shallow life is when it is lived merely for the pleasure of the moment without any regard to the future or its consequences, for standing back and looking at their own lives, so that, like Scrooge when the ghosts of Christmas Past and Christmas Present and Christmas Future whisked him away, they will have a chance to mend their ways, to become wholesome, to become worthy, and to become children of God.

They need *the Christ of Christmas and renewal of their inner spirits*. That is what it all comes down to, isn't it? They need to hear and receive the message of Christmas, that God has entered

the human arena to dwell with us, th
ence is consequently here and ava
now, that we are not alone, spinr
destinies on this third-rate planet abou. ... ..
blown up by our own brilliant stupidity, and
that all our days are spent before the Holy One
of Israel who poured all that He was and is and
will be through the funnel of a miracle into the
child born in the manger of Bethlehem. They
need to surrender their lives to Christ, who is
the real Gift of Christmas, and in the end He so
overshadows all others as to be the only one.

They—we—for in a sense I am talking about
all of us.

The late Dr. David Roberts, a psychotherapist,
told a story he had read somewhere of a French
soldier who suffers from amnesia. His face had
been horribly disfigured by a shell blast at the
front, and all his identification was blown away.
When he recovers from his injuries, there is no
way of telling who he is. The social services lo-
cates three possible families he might belong to,
on the basis of his general physical description,
and makes arrangements for him to visit each of
the families, in different parts of the country, to
see if the families recognize him. The first two
visits end sadly with no glint of recognition on
either side. When he steps off the train in the
third village, something about the station and
its environment seem familiar. As he walks

down the street, it all begins to come back, and he turns this way and that, growing increasingly surer of where he is, until he arrives at the cottage where his family lives and knows that he is home.

That is the way it ought to be for us at Christmas. Most of us have been lost in the busyness of our existence, trying to cope from day to day, and have quite forgotten who we are—or whose we are. But as we draw nearer to Christmas, and pass through the familiar landmarks of the season, we should begin to remember our real identities, until, coming down to Christmas Eve itself, we know that we are home, home where we belong, in the loving arms of God. And then we, who thought we had everything, realize we have nothing, and, realizing we have nothing, stand ready to receive everything. For He is our joy and peace.

In all the frenzy and noise of the season, O God, help us to find our way home; and, having found it, let us never lose it. Through Christ, who was born to show us the way. Amen.

10

Room for a King

History has been rather hard on the poor inn-keeper of the Christmas story, hasn't it? He is almost always portrayed as an insensitive lout or a dolt, a man who missed his one great opportunity in life. Here was Mary ready to give birth in Bethlehem, and this stupid oaf of an innkeeper didn't realize it and sent the family around to the stable behind the inn!

But we obviously overplay the scene. It was no Holiday Inn he was managing, with five thousand square feet of lounge and entertainment space, two hundred rooms and a heated swimming pool. It was a simple country inn, rough and unpretentious. There were perhaps four or five rooms at most in a town virtually swollen with guests.

The innkeeper's crime, if any, was small.

And there is a worse crime, that many of us who sit in judgment on this ancient innkeeper have not really made room for Christ in our lives; or, if we have, we have given Him, at best, a mere stable.

Let me take you for a moment from the Christmas story to another story, much later, over in the Book of Revelation. John, the author of the book, explained why he wrote it. It was the Lord's day, he said, and he was dwelling in the Spirit—something we all ought to do on the Lord's day!—when suddenly a voice sounded like a trumpet behind him, saying, "Write what you see in a book and send it to the seven churches." He turned to see where the voice was coming from, and the Lord Himself was there. He was dressed in a long robe tied at the waist with a golden belt. His face and His hair were as white as snow, and His eyes were like two burning flames. His feet had the appearance of burnished bronze, as if refined in a furnace, and His voice, said John, was like the rolling of the ocean. John was struck down by fear. He had never seen anything like it. But the Lord reached down and touched him. "Do not be afraid;" He said, "It is I, *The first* and *the Last; I* am the Living One, I was dead and now I am to live for ever and ever, and I hold the keys of death and of the underworld. Now write down all that you see of present happenings and *things that are still to come*" (Rev. 1:17-19, JB). And John did. The Book of Revelation consists of things that were happening then and of things that were yet to come.

One of the churches to which John wrote his book was the church at Laodicea. "Write to the angel of the church of Laodicea," said the Lord. "Here is the message of the Amen, the faithful, the true witness, the ultimate source of God's creation: I know all about you: how you are neither cold nor hot. I wish you were one or the other, but since you are neither, but only lukewarm, I will spit you out of my mouth" (3:14-16, JB). You think you are rich, said the Lord, because you have made fortunes and can afford to buy everything you want. But you are really "wretchedly and pitiably poor, and blind and naked too. I warn you, buy from me the gold that has been tested in the fire to make you really rich, and white robes to clothe you and cover your shameful nakedness, and eye ointment to put on your eyes so that you are able to see" (3:17-18, JB). I discipline those I love, said the Lord, so you had better get on your knees and change your ways.

Wow! That's something, isn't it? It sends a tremor through us, like an approaching earthquake. Rich! Able to buy everything we want, or almost everything. And He disciplines those He loves!

But wait, there's more.

"Look," said the Lord, still addressing the

church at Laodicea, "I am standing at the door, knocking. If one of you hears me calling and opens the door, I will come in to share his meal, side by side with him" (3:20, JB).

If *one* of you hears me calling. . . . not, if the whole town hears. Not if the whole church hears. Not even if your whole Sunday School class hears. But "if *one* of you hears me calling and opens the door, I will come in to share his meal, side by side with him."

Intimacy with Christ. How many of us have it? Christ sharing our meals, side by side with us at the table . . . .? And we think the innkeeper in Bethlehem was guilty.

I have seen Holman Hunt's famous painting *The Light of the World* in Keble College, Oxford, which was inspired by this story in Revelation. It is a haunting sermon in oils. The day is gone. It is supper time. Christ—luminous, radiant— stands before the door of the cottage, His hand raised in the act of knocking. There is no latch on the outside of the door. The person on the inside completely controls the entryway. That is true to life, isn't it? *We* decide whether Christ will come into our lives. *We* hold the mastery of the door, and no one else holds it for us—not Christ, not the church, not our parents, not anyone.

Christ does not force His way into our lives. The disciples wanted to be forceful with the gospel. When they came upon a village that would not receive the Lord, they said, "Let's call down fire out of heaven and consume these people!" But Jesus rebuked the disciples and went on to another town. He never forces entry.

There was no force used at Bethlehem. God came to earth as a little Infant crying in the night—inconspicuous, unsuspected. No force at all.

Isn't that the way God still comes into our lives? And we often miss Him because we are too wrapped up in other things, as the innkeeper of Bethlehem doubtless was—too much business, too much homework, too much shopping, too many parties. He comes, and we miss Him. We would weep at the tragedy, if we thought about it, if we were smart enough to know what we had missed.

"A March morning," wrote Aldo Leopold in *A Sand County Almanac*, "is only as drab as he who walks in it without a glance skyward, ear cocked for geese. I once knew an educated lady, banded by Phi Beta Kappa, who told me that she had never heard or seen the geese that twice a year proclaim the revolving seasons to her well-insulated roof. Is education possibly a process of trading awareness for things of lesser worth?"

And God is so much more important than geese!

"If one of you hears me calling and opens the

door," says Christ, "I will come in to share his meal, side by side with him" (JB). "I will come in to him, and will sup with him," the King James Version says. He doesn't expect an elaborate meal. You don't have to prepare it ahead of time and sweep and decorate the cottage as well. He comes and knocks and takes potluck. It is a quiet affair, without trumpets and fanfare. It may be that He arrives after we have turned out the lights and gone to bed and there is only a pot of soup on the stove. It doesn't matter. The important thing is sharing it with Him. It is a beautiful picture of friendship.

I wish Holman Hunt had painted a sequel to his great painting. I wish he had painted a picture with two persons, one of them Christ and the other the person living in the cottage, sitting in the warm glow from the fireplace in the kitchen and sipping from a bowl of soup or gruel, maybe with a dog curled at their feet, contented to be in the Master's presence. Perhaps the glow would be coming from Christ and not from the fireplace—or from the lowly cottage dweller, who is so happy and satisfied that he is literally radiant. In any event, it would be a gentle, peaceful scene, full and beautiful and moving.

But perhaps this quiet meeting with Christ is not all the story. It may begin that way, peacefully enough, but it doesn't always remain that way, does it? The small stable of Bethlehem was

soon burgeoning with other figures, wasn't it?
Shepherds, the Magi, and heaven knows who
else. The King of kings brings His retinue, doesn't He? And that must be reckoned with.

It was always that way with royalty. Royalty
never really comes alone. My wife and I once
visited the famous country estate of Longleat in
southern England. It was built in the late six-
teenth century by Sir John Thynne, and the gar-
dens were designed by a well-known landscapist
named "Capability" Brown. Shortly after the
great house was completed, Sir John was hon-
ored by a visit from Queen Elizabeth I. It nearly
ruined him! The queen came with hundreds of
her court, and she found the house so pleasant
that she stayed for several days. Imagine hous-
ing and feeding all those people!

They say the scene was similar at the White
House when Andrew Jackson was sworn in as
the seventh president of the United States. All
the Tennesseans who knew Jackson and all the
old soldiers who had fought with him at New
Orleans came to Washington and descended on
the White House. They devoured the food,
tracked mud into all the rooms, swung on the
drapes, spat tobacco juice on the carpets, and
generally ruined the furniture.

And I must warn you that it is the experience
of those who open their hearts to Christ that He
almost never comes alone into a life. There are

dozens, perhaps hundreds, of poor, infirm, illiterate souls that accompany Him. All those starving children in Ethiopia and the Sudan, and the disease-ridden tribespeople of the southwest United States, the crowds of Hindus in India, and the snobbish intellectuals in the universities. Do we have room in our hearts for them as well? And school children on drugs, and dirty, old men and women on the streets? He will bring them, I promise you. He always does. It is His way. His "little ones," He calls them. And He says that whatever we do for them is done for Him. "Inasmuch as you have done it for the least of these . . . you have done it for me."

It's enough to make you want to keep the door shut, isn't it? Unless you are lonely. Unless you know there is something missing in your life. It is almost Christmas. Our lives are crowded as usual. There are so many parties to go to, so many gifts to purchase and wrap. There is so much decorating to do, cleaning, and cooking. It is easy to miss Christ in all of it—or to send Him to a stable. We know. We've done it before, at other Christmases. He won't crash our parties or force Himself on us. He won't plant Himself in front of the Christmas tree and demand to be noticed. But we can watch for Him and let Him in if we want to. We can listen for His voice and open the door to Him—if we're willing to make room for His friends as well.

If we don't, the Judge in heaven may say that we were worse than the innkeeper of Bethlehem. You see, He hadn't heard the gospel, and we have. We *know* the King of kings is at the door. We don't have the innkeeper's excuse.

O Lord, who is content in the smallest hovel where You are truly welcome, help us to throw wide the doors of our hearts and bid You to come in this Christmas—with all your little ones, who would also have a place in our lives. For your blessed name's sake. Amen.

11

Pardon My Breakdown

Somehow the story of the Gadarene demoniac seems appropriate for the Sunday after Christmas. How many of us understand the demoniac better today than we did a month ago! Christmas is beautiful and uplifting, and year after year we manage to find the strength for it. But when it is over, many of us are sympathetic with the woman in the cartoon gleefully jumping up and down on her Christmas tree and all the presents under it, or with the department store Santa on his way home on Christmas Eve who snarls at a little child in its parents' arms and makes it cry. Basically, we have a problem of overload—of putting too much pressure on our systems. In our mystery-starved technological world, we tend to overdo for Christmas. Then we pay the price for it.

Doctors and psychiatrists have noted for years that there is always a bloody aftermath to Christmas. Perhaps we should call it "Herod's

Syndrome," for the massacre that followed the birth of the Child in Bethlehem. Some persons become physically ill from the stress they have undergone. Others suffer from depression; the strain of all the excitement, of coping with memories and money problems and family situations, becomes too much for them. There is even a marked increase in the incidence of suicide, usually among persons who could not bear the contrast between the high idealism of the Christmas season and the ugly realities of their own existence.

It may seem ironic that the birthday of the Prince of peace should become the occasion for such widespread distress. But actually this is only symptomatic of the human situation and ought not to add to our burden of guilt by making us feel that we are worse than we are. It is a fact of life that there are rhythms to our behavior—ebbs and flows, surges and withdrawals—and some of us merely go to more excess in our rhythms than others. When the balance in our natures gets upset, it must be restored.

There is, therefore, a kind of sanity to breakdowns, if you think about it. They are the compensating factors in our lives. They may restore balance when we have let our emphases get out of resonance. Was it Chesterton who said that the only sane people he knew were in institutions? Something in us wonders, the week after

Christmas, if the man in our Scripture wasn't smarter than the townspeople who said he was possessed of a demon. At least, there are times when we would all feel better if we could have an old-fashioned breakdown, if we could throw off the restraints of clothing, roll around in the dust, and rail at anybody who tried to come near us.

We don't know why the Gadarene was out of phase with society. The Scriptures don't provide such information. We know he didn't have too much Christmas, but if he were Jewish, it is possible that he had had too much Passover or Hanukkah. If he came from a well-to-do home, where education was valued, he may have had too much educational pressure. Counselors in schools will tell you that this often happens, especially in high-powered private academies and topflight universities. Students compensate in their rhythms by failing or dropping out. There is another possibility, that the man succumbed to the pressures of married life and a family. I always cringe when counseling with people about to marry at the thoughts of the pressures they are letting themselves in for. They cannot possibly know, in the stages of courtship and early marriage, how difficult the way will be in places. Yet again, the man in the story may have suffered from business pressures. I think of the people in our congregation who have to struggle

with rising inflation and the hopeless entangle-
ments of bureaucracy and government interfer-
ence; I wonder that they are able to keep their
balance at all.

What I would like you to see, quite apart from
the Scripture, which will hardly bear such ex-
egesis, is that there is nothing abnormal about
breakdowns. They are the way we compensate
for imbalance in our lives. Some of us compensate by having a lot of little breakdowns along
the way. Others, perhaps like the man in our
story, resist the little breakdowns and then,
when they finally have one, have a lollapalooza.

I myself give in to little breakdowns, momen-
tary lapses in my otherwise rather sedate and
decorous behavior. I think of them as the bits
and pieces of comic relief in a serious play that
drain off tension and make the plot manageable.
Sometimes they amount to no more than taking
an afternoon off to go for a walk or read a book.
Occasionally they assume a more dramatic as-
pect, like the one that occurred in Colorado.

We were camping in the Rockies. One afternoon we hiked up into the mountains, following
the trail of a little trout stream. Somewhat in
advance of my wife and boys, I came upon a
breathtaking stretch of meadow, hidden high in
the hills. Daisies and columbines grew in wild
profusion among the grass. Thousands of white
butterflies danced above them, giving the im-

pression that the flowers themselves were frolicking in the sunlight. Overcome by the unexpectedness of all that natural beauty, I had a little breakdown and gamboled like a spring lamb across that meadow. Kris was the first one into the clearing behind me. "Mom!" he shouted. "Come quick! Dad's gone crazy!"

Not crazy-crazy. Just one of my little breakdowns. Part of my way of coping, of staying sane.

But, if part of our humanity is getting into excesses and having to have breakdowns, part of God's divinity is God's steadiness and reliability, God's never having to have breakdowns. That is the other side of the coin. It is human to have breakdowns. It is divine not to.

This doesn't mean that we ought to be divine and not have any breakdowns. That would be the improper conclusion. We know this because it is the conclusion the Pharisees drew about human existence. They were always on the lookout for people's lapses or breakdowns. Jesus pilloried them for all time in the portrait of the Pharisees at prayer, who said, before the steadiness and reliability of God, "I thank thee, that I am not as other men are" (Luke 18:11, KJV). We have never liked pharisaism in anyone, because it is not a comely picture of humanity. It is too tight, too arrogant, and too self-serving. This is why one of the ageless devices of comedy has always been to show something ridiculous happening to the self-righteous person; he is slammed in the face with a custard pie, falls down a flight of stairs, or slips on a banana peel. We laugh at the redressing of an imbalance in human nature. We would all like to throw custard pies in the faces of priggish moralists, stuffy professors, and social bigots. We want to humiliate them—to bring them back to the *humis*, back to earth.

But how comforting it is to think of the steadiness of God: He is my rock and my salvation (Ps. 89: 26). Knowing that, we are able to live with our own frailties, our excesses, our need for breakdowns. "Underneath are the everlasting arms" (Deut. 33:27, KJV). That frees us to be human.

God is the cure for our imbalances. That is why, in church, we are always talking about the importance of prayer and meditation. It is not because our needles are stuck on a particular way of speaking. It is because God's steadiness and dependability are the antithesis of our instability and because it is healthy for us to be in the presence of God.

Did you ever read Samuel Butler's famous novel *The Way of All Flesh*? The main character in the story, Ernest Pontifex, is a young ministerial candidate who has a nervous breakdown. In his case, the breakdown occurs because he is caught between two opposing views of life and religion—an older, traditionalist view and a newer, more liberal way of looking at things. Do you remember when the breakdown has occurred what a wise doctor recommends to Pontifex as a cure? He sends him to the zoo to watch the elephants. That's right, the elephants. And the prescription works. Standing daily before the great pachyderms and watching them pad slowly and methodically from side to side in their pits, Pontifex feels a new rhythm being established in his being. It is slower, more deliberate, than his old rhythm. It steadies him. He gradually finds his balance again in the ageless balance of the great beasts.

So we find our balance again in God—a cure for the madness in our hearts, for imbalance in our passions, and for the excesses in our behavior. In God's eternal, unchanging consistency, we find a new rhythm for ourselves.

This was the remarkable thing about Jesus. He lived so completely in the presence of the Father that there was always an exquisite balance in His life. What steadiness and composure He manifested! Even in the face of torture and death, His inner purpose burned with the steadiness of an eternal flame.

What did Tournier write about him? That if ever there was a man with a reason to seem harried or fatigued, it was Jesus. He was always on the road to someplace, always dealing with crowds, always under the pressure of enemies trying to ensnare Him. Yet, when we read the Gospels, what do we see? A man of luminous calm. A man who always had time for children or for people who were hurting. A man with time for prayer.

There was the secret, of course. He always had time for prayer. His life was a rhythm of activity and prayer, prayer and activity. He worked among the masses, healing, teaching, debating, and then retiring to pray. Always the reciprocity was there—work and prayer, life and God.

And, out of that abundance of health, Jesus brought new life to people who had broken down. In the text, he drove the demons out of a man into a herd of swine—a fit place for such excesses. Swine are known as beasts of excess. Better the demons in them than in human beings—though even they were unable to bear it. When the townspeople came out, they found the healed man sitting calmly on a rock. His life was back in order. It was time for the townspeople to show their insanity: They asked Jesus to leave the area.

Here is our word for the postholiday: Rely upon God for your balance. It is not abnormal to have a breakdown—that will be pardoned. But the way of Christmas—what Christmas was really intended to teach us—is that God is the secret at the heart of human success. God is the unchanging One by whom we reestablish a saving rhythm in our lives.

If you have overdone, if you are exhausted by your preparations for Christmas, if the stresses are too much for you, there is a good word for you. God is dependable. God is eternal. If you will come regularly into His presence, the way a person walks out each evening to the end of a peninsula and stands for an hour, absorbing the rhythm of the sea, you will take on the balance of God in your own life.

There is one more note. When the man in the Scripture had been cured of his breakdown, he was so excited about Jesus that he wanted to follow Him everywhere. He wanted to "professionalize" his experience. But Jesus said no. Go back to your people, Jesus said, and be a witness there. Let them see in you the kind of sanity that testifies to the goodness of God.

We are tempted, as this man was, to make a lifetime out of one experience. Having found salvation, even for a moment, we want to overdo that, too, and to get away from life where we have lived it. But the witness of Jesus is that we are not to get away, that we are to live out our humanity where we are. Our real calling is to be human, not to be divine. And, as Sam Keen has said, "To be human means keeping at least one foot firmly rooted in Boaz, Alabama, or some such improbable point of incarnation."

So, like the demoniac, we return to the life that is always threatened by imbalances and breakdowns. That is our lot. But we return knowing the Name that is able to frighten our demons. We return knowing the One in whose presence there is eternal steadiness.

O Lord of all nature, even of our unsteadiness, help us to submit ourselves to You so completely that Your thoughts become our thoughts and Your rhythms our rhythms, now and forever. Through Jesus Christ our Lord. Amen.

12

Losing the Star

An indisposition following Christmas allowed me time to review our many Christmas cards and reflect on the variety of images by which we greet each other at this season of the year. There were the usual crèche scenes, Santa Clauses, and poinsettias. There were also a number of redbirds, reindeer, and soft, furry little animals, some playing in the snow and some gathering around the infant Christ. But the figures that won out again, hands down, as they seem to Christmas after Christmas, were the Wise Men, those indefatigable, saddle-sore creatures from the mysterious lands of the East with names like Rampur, Bangalore, and Samarkand. They have ridden across more miles for Hallmark and American Greeting Cards than they ever rode to get to Bethlehem! And invariably they follow the star, a great luminous body whose brilliance both vents and vexes the geometrical skills of the cards' designers. The Wise Men would not be the Wise Men without their wondrous star.

Or would they?

It occurred to me this year, for the first time in a lifetime of reading the Christmas accounts in the Gospels, that much of their journey that first Christmas was made without benefit of the star. They saw the star in the East, shining with incredible brightness over their homelands, and they saw it again as they left the palace of Herod. But in between, encompassing the vast distance from where their journey began to the few miles that marked its conclusion, I believe they were without its benefit much of the way. This is why they stopped off at Herod's palace. The star had guided them in the general direction of the little nation of Israel, but then it seemed to desert them and leave them on their own. They went to the court of Herod, assuming that the astrologers of the court could aid them in solving the riddle of the star. And then, as they left the court, the star mysteriously appeared again, this time guiding them to the unlikely stable in Bethlehem.

Talk about realism! Isn't that the way it happens with all of us? We have our moments of seeing and knowing, when the star of clarity and certainty goes before us, and then nothing. Everything seems to go blank; somebody throws a hat down on our jigsaw puzzle, and it's back to confusion and desperation. My life is like that, isn't yours? I remember when I was about ten years old and went to my first midnight movie. It was a horror film called *Frankenstein Meets the Werewolf.* And then I had to walk home by myself, through the darkest, most terrifying night I have ever known. The only comfort on the way was the presence of streetlights. I felt safe in the light. When I got under a streetlight, I strolled as if I had all the time in the world. Then I dashed off like a championship sprinter to the next light. And I have often thought that all life is like that, making our way from one light to the next, with darkness for the rest of the way. That is what the Wise Men did. They traveled from one sighting of the star to the next. They didn't see it constantly. They had to travel long distances without it.

What can we learn from these Wise Men and their vagrant star?

First, we learn that life is a journey. Life isn't rootedness, and it isn't settledness. It is journey, movement, going from one place to another. The minute we think we've got it all settled, tied up, or nailed down, it springs loose on us and begins to unravel. Haven't you noticed that? Perhaps this is why the greatest writers have always depicted life as a pilgrimage, a movement from one place to another. From Geoffrey Chaucer to James Michener, from Dante to Bernard Malamud, it is the same in every age: Life is a journey, a progressing of mind and heart and body.

Part of my Christmas reading has been William Least Heat Moon's marvelous saga of American life called *Blue Highways: A Journey into America.* It begins when the author is released from his teaching responsibilities at a college in Missouri. With a little over four hundred dollars and an old Ford van named Ghost Dancing, he sets out to see America and to do it by following only the smaller highways, the ones colored blue on the highway maps. The journey takes him into many of the smaller towns and unknown rural areas of the country —places like Bug, Kentucky, and Nameless, Tennessee—and brings him into contact with some of the "real" people of America, such as Rosemary and Bill Hammond, who spent more than six years building an all-steel boat in the basin of the Kentucky River; and Miss Ginny Watts, who had kept a death book with twenty years' worth of entries of names she had heard on the radio and found in the newspapers in her part of Tennessee. As you read a book like *Blue Highways*, you begin to envy the author for seeing so much. Then you realize that all life is the same way: It is a journey where we see and learn things.

Eventually, if you are lucky, you see that the important stance in life, the most important way to be, is openness. It is realizing that life is gift and that those persons receive most who are poised to receive. This is the way it was with the Wise Men; they followed the star that appeared in their sky. They were open and ready to be led. They knew that life is an adventure, and those see most who are most ready to follow.

The second thing we learn from the Wise Men is that faith is what we exercise in times of darkness. Faith is for the times of the journey when we can't see the star. What does the Letter to the Hebrews say? "Now faith is the substance of things hoped for, the evidence of things not seen" (Heb. 11:1, KJV). Contrary to the pictures on the Christmas cards, the Wise Men traveled long miles of their journey in the dark, without benefit of the glorious star. The star got them started on their journey, and it returned when the journey was at its climax, but in between, over miles and miles of barren and even hostile countryside, it appeared to leave them. It was there all the time, of course, but they could not see it. They had to journey onward in the direction it had given them, but without its immediate aid.

This too is true to life, isn't it? We spend a lot of our journeys in the dark. We see the star shining over a certain college, and we go there, not knowing what lies beyond for us. We see it shining again over a career or a profession, and we go in that direction, not knowing any more than that. Again and again in life, we have a moment of great luminosity, when everything becomes clear and we feel affirmed in our choices; then the light gives way to great stretches of darkness, when we must walk alone, with only the memory of the light to guide us.

A woman went to her counselor and wept a great deal because she felt so uncertain about her life's direction at that moment of her pilgrimage. The counselor, undismayed by the tears, said, "My dear, surely you have lived long enough to realize that life is like this. There are times of light and times of darkness. One always gives way to the other."

And that is true, isn't it? The star does not shine brightly at all times. When it doesn't, we must walk by faith, by recollections of its shining and by hope in its shining again. We cannot, in our finitude, expect it to shine for us all the time. Even the disciples of Jesus, when He was crucified, lost their bearings in the darkness. But their star came out again.

I shall never forget a visit I had once in the hospital with a dear friend of ours who is a nun. She had pneumonia, but that was not the worst thing. The worst thing, she said, was that in her illness she found herself unable to pray. "But that is all right," she said. "I have prayed before, and I shall pray again. Right now, I must learn to wait."

And so must we all learn to wait when the star is not shining. We have seen it before; we shall see it again. But in the interim there is nothing to do but to keep going on the journey and wait until it appears again.

One more thing we learn from the Wise Men: At the end of the journey is Christ. In terms of our Christian experience, at least, we may have thought He was at the beginning of the journey. But He is also at the end, in a way that is now almost too marvelous to anticipate. "Let us run with perseverance," said the writer of Hebrews, "the race that is set before us, looking to Jesus the pioneer and perfecter of our faith" (12:1-2). Though the journey was often couched in darkness, the Wise Men found Christ at the end. And there was no question about the journey's being worth it. That is good news to those who are in a darkened phase of their life's journeys, isn't it? When you have lost the star, hold on; you will come out on the other end of the darkness, and there will be light you cannot now believe.

At Notre Dame University, there is a great mosaic of Christ, several stories tall, on the side of the library building. He stands with His arms outspread and lifted and is clearly visible from the football stadium. The students long ago nicknamed Him "Touchdown Jesus." Touchdown Jesus. That's the gospel in a nutshell, isn't it? Jesus at the end of all our struggles, ready to say, "You made it!" And His being there makes all the journey different. Knowing He is there, we can endure our seasons of darkness and our times of pain. Knowing He is there, we can make it through the hardships. Knowing He is there, we can survive even loss and death. For we know we shall hear Him say, "Well done, good and faithful servant. You made it!"

A friend of mine described the death of her father after long months of battling against cancer. He had been through the ordeal of surgery and chemotherapy, and in the final weeks most of his body had wasted away as his abdomen grew larger and larger. At the end he entered a semi-coma, emerging only occasionally to greet some relative or friend waiting with him in the room. And she was there, my friend was there, when on one of these occasions he came around, reached for her hand, and announced, "I see my Savior. He has been there all the time."

That is what our faith is all about: He has been there all the time. Through all the darkness and all the struggles, past all the pitfalls and all the valleys, He is there. And that is what sustains all wise men and women on their journeys.

Show us Yourself, O Lord, and no way is too long or journey too hazardous for us to undertake. But reveal yourself as the Light at the end of the way, and we shall follow You through death itself. For You hold eternal life in Your hands. Amen.

13

The Trip After Christmas

On the Sunday before Christmas newspapers were crammed with advertisements for journeys we are invited to make now that Christmas is over. There are trips to Acapulco, Trinidad, Rio, and Miami; Maui, Aspen, New York, and Las Vegas; London, Rome, and Torremolinos. Or, for the less well heeled, there are briefer excursions to Atlantic City, Williamsburg, and Tyson's Corner. Somebody apparently thinks we are awfully sick of leftover turkey, drooping trees, and the frightful mess our houses are in!

Or perhaps the travel agents all recognize some theological significance about making trips after Christmas because Jesus and the holy family, being directed by an angel, journeyed into Egypt after the birth in Bethlehem.

But of that journey we are driven to ask why. Why did the angel tell Joseph to take Mary and Jesus and travel south into Egypt? It was a long and difficult journey, especially when undertaken with a newborn child and on top of the already arduous journey they had made from Galilee to Bethlehem. Oh, one reason is obvious, of course; Herod, the mad old monarch, was sending out his soldiers to slay all the male children under two years of age, supposing he might thereby write *finis* to the purposes of God. That would be reason enough. But the Scriptures are always inviting us back for a second look, for a glimpse into some deeper purpose, into the heart of some mystery hidden from the hurried viewer. What other explanations could there be for this puzzling excursion, that is mentioned but once in the Gospels and there but scantly, in a mere three verses?

Some commentator, I do not doubt, will find in the Egyptian trip a reference to Moses, the great leader of the Jews who was born in Egypt and hidden, like Jesus, from the despotic powers that would have slain him. Matthew, in whose account our text occurs, was concerned all the way through the Gospel to draw out relationships between Jesus and Moses, and to show, beyond any reasonable doubt, the superiority of Jesus over the revered Jewish leader of the past. The Sermon on the Mount in Matthew parallels Moses' going into the heights of Sinai to bring down the Law the the people of Israel. When Jesus was transfigured that night on the mountain and appeared in conversation with Moses and Elijah, it was of Jesus that the voice of God announced, "This is my beloved Son, with whom I am well pleased" (Matt. 3:17). And when the Pharisees taunted Jesus on the subject of divorce, He said that Moses allowed it only because their hearts were hardened, but this expediency was not what God really wanted (Matt. 19:8). Jesus was clearly number one, Moses was number two, and the trip into Egypt was a way of establishing the relationship before rubbing it in.

But the real clue is probably in the text Matthew quoted in verse 15, "Out of Egypt have I called my son." God sent the holy family into Egypt to fulfill this Scripture. The text first occurs in the ancient prophetic Book of Hosea in the Old Testament. The full text says:

> When Israel was a child, I loved him,
>   and out of Egypt I called my son.
> The more I called them,
>   the more they went from me;
> they kept sacrificing to the Baals,
>   and burning incense to idols (11:1-2).

[handwritten margin note: ref. to Israel not messiah! ?]

It is a text that turns from tender to fierce. God remembers His early dealings with the Israelites and how much He loved them. He is like a father grieving for what might have been. Then He remembers their infidelities, the way they took His gifts and squandered them, pros-

tituting themselves to false gods, and His speech
turns cold and hard and full of anger.

Jesus and the holy family made the journey
into Egypt, in Matthew's Gospel, as a symbolic
act encompassing His relationship to Israel and
the judgment He would bring, as the new Israel,
upon the old regime. Like Israel of old, Jesus
was the beloved Son of God; and when He grew
to manhood, His followers would displace the
old Israel as heirs of the kingdom.

What we have here, then, is a very significant
journey. It is not a mere incidental part of the
Christmas story, an appendage to be glossed
over and forgotten. It is a retracing of the very
steps of the old Israel by the new and, therefore,
a prophetic word about the ministry of Christ.
Like ancient Israel, He sojourned in the land of
slavery, traveled through the land of wilderness,
and entered the Land of Promise.

The land of slavery. How appropriate that the
life of Christ should very early establish contact
with the land of slavery. In a sense, all our journeys begin in the land of slavery, don't they?
Freud understood this. We live at the mercy of
our impulses, he said. They constitute a great
inner core of our nature and drive us all our
lives. We try to get the better of them by forming
part of the mind as a kind of moral guard to keep
the slave in check. But guards have a way of

becoming prisoners, in a manner of speaking. We only choose different ways of being slaves.

Sometimes the slavery is more obvious. I flew into a midwestern city a few weeks ago, enroute to a preaching mission. I was met at the airport by a gentleman whose benefaction had made the mission possible. The mission was named for his son, who had died in a motorcycle crash five years earlier. On the way to the town where the mission was held, he poured out his story.

At the time when the son was killed, a daughter was wasting her life with drugs and booze. She spent several weeks at an expensive care center, but the cure lasted only a few days. Two years later, he received a phone call from the police in Minnesota. His daughter had been arrested for drunken driving and was in jail. He thanked the officer but said she would have to get out on her own; he understood enough about her addiction to know that he could not make things all right for her. Three months later the officer called again. The daughter had served her time. If the father would come get her and find a job for her, she would be released. She owed a thousand dollars to the state of Minnesota and must pay it out of her earnings within the next six months. I met the daughter. She had been sober for six months and had just finished paying her fine. She was beginning to rebuild her broken life.

"How did you stand it, losing your son and knowing how things were with your daughter at the same time?" I asked. "I thought I would lose my mind," he said. "But then I had a religious experience. I can't describe it. It was as if Christ put His hand on my shoulder and His touch transformed me. Everything was different after that. I was the lowest I had ever been—lower than I ever thought it possible to be—and then everything turned around."

I looked over at his gentle face in the light of the oncoming headlights. A soft rain was falling, and sometimes the water gathered on the windshield and made shadows on his face. There had been a lot of pain on that face over the years. But now the pain was gone, and there was only gentleness and love. *His* slavery was over, at least. The Christ who was carried at birth into the land of slavery had delivered him as surely as God once delivered the Israelites.

The land of wilderness. After Egypt, the desert. Barren, lonely, threatening. Hiding place of thieves and murderers. Confusing and easy to get lost in, even today. Especially then. Joseph probably made contact with a caravan, some band of itinerant merchants, and traveled with them for the safety of his family. Inexperienced people did not tackle the wilderness alone.

Even when we escape from slavery, the wilderness is still there, isn't it? Even after the saving experience of Christ, there is still the journey, with all its windings and turnings, its pitfalls and hard times, its periods of desolation and despair. Don't be ashamed of them. They are part of life. Being a Christian doesn't exempt you from them, anymore than it exempts you from flu and stubbed toes and the backache.

One of the beautiful things about reading Christian biographies is the way the authors pull back the veil and let you look into their times of hurt and awkwardness and failure. Then you know that everybody has such times. I enjoyed reading Wayne Oates's autobiography *The Struggle to Be Free*. Wayne is one of the fathers of the modern pastoral care movement and a great Christian pastor and professor. Years ago, in his first pastorate, he wrote, he became quite ill and went to the doctor. The doctor told him he was eating too many fried foods and had to give them up. Then the doctor said, "There's something else wrong too." Puzzled, Wayne asked what it was. "You are a young pastor," said the doctor. "You are trying too hard. You are trying to be Jesus. It won't work. He's already gotten there first. You are just one of his men putting in a good word for him. Keep doing that, but don't try to replace him. It can't be done" (p. 131). All his life, Wayne has struggled to be free, to be somebody, to do well. He will go on struggling because life itself is a wilderness we all traverse.

But the wonderful fact is that the Christ who was carried through the wilderness as an infant still leads His people through the wilderness areas of life. Wherever we are in the wilderness, we have but to pause and listen, and we will hear Him speak. He is always with us.

I had a letter before Christmas from Khiem Lac Tran, our Vietnamese friend who migrated to San Diego recently with his family. They have had a difficult autumn. Neither of the adult Trans speaks English. They had very little money. Only recently was Lac able to find work. But he wrote a glowing, beautiful letter. "It was hard fall," he said, "and we have many difficulties. But our Lord is always with us, making things better. We give thanks for him and for our friends in Lynchburg. Our family will always rejoice in his love."

He is Lord over slavery, and He is Lord of the wilderness.

And, finally, *the Land of Promise*. Joseph and Mary must have felt as glad to see it again as those first Israelites who arrived at the Jordan River and looked over at the walls of Jericho. It was home. It was safety. It was fulfillment. It was the place where the redemption of the world would be accomplished. It was the end of the journey.

What would life be without the Land of Promise at the end of it? How could we bear our burdens if it were not there? A hymn by Samuel Stennett that many of us love goes like this:

I am bound for the promised land,
I am bound for the promised land;
O who will come and go with me?
I am bound for the promised land.

How many people, lonely, tired, sick, and discouraged have sung that song and derived comfort and strength from its vision? The Land of Promise? And Christ is Lord of the land of promise. He is Lord over slavery and Lord over the wilderness and the Lord of fulfillment.

Many persons who have had the so-called "life-after-life" experiences, of floating out of the body and being "dead" for a matter of minutes, have reported that Jesus was the first person they encountered in the beyond. Maybe, retorts the cynic, that is because it was Jesus they expected to see. That is possible. Or maybe it is because they were experiencing our deepest reality. Now is Jesus become the "firstfruits of them that slept," said Paul (1 Cor. 15:20, KJV). He is the "head of the body" (Col. 1:18). And since that is so—since it was *Truth* that was revealed to the earliest Christians—then He *is* Lord of the promise, and He will be waiting to greet us when we disembark on the other side of life.

Do you wish to know what the Promised Land will be like? Then look to Christ. It is His land.

He is the Lord of it. It will reflect His graciousness, His intelligence, His love. It will be a land where children sit on the knee and play in contentment. It will be a land where all sickness is cured and all blindness turned to sight. It will be a land where honesty and justice prevail without compromise, where all the broken and little folk of the world will at last enjoy full equality and reparation. It will be a land where the miracle is ordinary and the water tastes like the finest wine. It will be a land of intimacy and growth and challenge, where we shall sit at the feet of the greatest Teacher the world has ever seen. And it shall be a land of love and unity, where the Judases shall have absented themselves and all that are left around the table of our Lord are of a single, sweet communion.

We have seen all of this in Christ. We shall see it even more beyond. For He is the Lord of our salvation.

O God, You are the Lord of all journeys, who willed that Christ be carried into Egypt and through the wilderness to the Promised Land again. Be Lord of our journeys too, that they may carry us into fellowship and fulfillment at the feet of Him who died and rose and reigns forever at Your side. Amen.

14

A Pattern for Worship in the New Year

The Magi almost slipped in and out of history without being noticed. They probably would have done so had it not been the Prince of peace Himself they came to see. We know almost nothing at all about them. Legend treats them as three Wise Men, though the Gospel does not specify their number. Eventually they were promoted to kings and given the names Melchior, Gaspar, and Balthasar. In 1158 three bodies were discovered in the Church of Saint Eustorgio in Milan, and local politicians conspired to identify them as those of the three Magi. A few years later Emperor Frederick Barbarossa captured the city and took the remains of the bodies to Germany, where they were laid to rest in Cologne Cathedral. Soon the shrine of the three kings became famous. It was one of the pilgrimage sites visited by Chaucer's Wife of Bath in *The Canterbury Tales*. Visitors to the cathedral are still shown the tombs of these men who were among the first to welcome Christ to earth, though now the guides generally wink when they tell the story.

Why did the writer of the Gospel bother to tell the story of their coming to the stable? He gave little real attention to it. What was his purpose in telling it at all?

For one thing, it emphasized the universal significance of Christ's birth. Whether the Magi were kings or mere Wise Men, the fact that they journeyed all the way from the East suggested that the birth of the Savior had an importance that reached far beyond the boundaries of little Judah. And there was the matter of the star that brought them. The star meant that the heavens themselves, the whole natural order of the universe, were in concert with God to accomplish the salvation of the world.

But maybe there was something else too. At least the early Christians, with their primitive way of seeing divine omens in casual events or reading important messages into apparently trivial occurrences, would have seen something else. They surely found in the sequence of events described in these scant verses of Matthew a pattern for the behavior of all who would come to the Prince of peace. Matthew said they came, they saw the Baby, they worshiped Him, and they presented Him with gifts. Could we ourselves, if we tried, invent a better plan for our worship in the new year?

Let's reflect on the pattern.

They came. Over a long distance, they came. Across alien terrain, they came. Without regard for the great obstacles, they came. Following a star of hope, they came. They came. That is the first requisite of worship, isn't it? We cannot worship if we do not come.

Oh, it is easy enough to say, "I can worship God as well in a boat on the lake or walking in the woods as I can in church," and it is certainly possible to feel the presence of God in these places. But there is something about coming to church—about making the effort—that prepares us for worship as nothing else does.

When I am retired and tempted some days not to go to worship, as we all are at times, I shall remember Mrs. Fannie Moore. Fannie is 101, and the law of gravity has had a whole century to overtake her now. Whenever I ask her on Sunday morning, "How are you, Fannie?" her reply has become a familiar ritual. "I didn't want to get up this morning," she says, "but I said to myself, 'Get up, old woman, and go to church.'" She knows the benefit of the discipline and the importance of attending church. It shapes our lives, even if we don't live to be 101.

A friend of mine was showing slides of his visit to Africa. "This is Tonga," he said, showing a photograph of a young woman he said was in her twenties. Tonga slept on a pallet in the back of the church she attended. She had shown up for worship one day and had sat wide eyed through the whole affair. Afterward, she hung around the church. "Aren't you going home?" asked one of the missionaries. "I cannot go home," she said. "My father said if I come to worship I should never return home."

Coming to worship has a significance all its own.

The Wise Men came, and *they saw*. Oh, what they saw! There are millionaires in the world today who would give every penny they possess to see what the Wise Men saw. That humble stable—the goats and the sheep—the simple maiden and her elderly husband—and the Child into whom had been poured the godhead itself! How plain the rest of the world must have looked to them after that—or how rich and beautiful. For that is the way with seeing the Christ, isn't it? It makes everything look different and beautiful.

Have you ever thought of what we do in church as "seeing"? That's really what it's about, isn't it? Seeing. Getting our sight adjusted. Having our eyes opened. If we come to church and go home and everything looks the same, it has been a pointless exercise. Things should look different after we have been worshiping the Lord.

Annie Dillard, who is something of our national expert on seeing, understands that there is a true connection between being in church and seeing. But she can't understand why most of us don't see more than we do. "Why do we people in churches," she asked, "seem like cheerful, brainless tourists on a packaged tour of the Absolute?" We deal with spiritual TNT, as if we were children playing on the floor with our chemistry sets. "It is madness to wear ladies' straw hats and velvet hats to church; we should all be wearing crash helmets. Ushers should issue life preservers and signal flares; they should lash us to our pews. For the sleeping god may wake someday and take offense, or the waking god may draw us out to where we can never return" (*Teaching a Stone to Talk*, pp. 40-41).

What a pity it is if we come to church without expecting anything and go home without having seen anything. For seeing—in the hymns, the prayers, the speech, the silences—is what it is all about.

The Wise Men came, they saw, and *they worshiped*. How could they resist? It is the natural movement once one has seen the Lord. When Thomas saw it in the upper room—saw that the Master who had been crucified that black day at Golgotha was really the risen Lord standing before him there in the little room where the disciples met, His nail-scarred hands held out in welcome to Thomas's doubting soul—Thomas fell to the floor and cried out, "My Lord and my God!" Did the Wise Men see something of this in the stable that day? The word of the Gospel is that they did. They came and saw and worshiped.

That ought to be the response when we see something in church, oughtn't it? It ought to be the response *wherever* we see something that turns our lives around or makes us feel more deeply about life. But especially in church. Worship is our response to the Word that became flesh and dwells among us.

It has happened to me in a hymn or an anthem. I will be sitting here by the pulpit listening to the choir, and some particular turn of phrase, some look on a choir member's face, some special chording of the organ, will open a hole in my consciousness a mile wide, and the light will flood in, stabbing my soul with joy. Tears will well up in my heart, and I will worship.

Once, before I came to this church, I was talking with a search committee from the First Congregational Church of Los Angeles. There was a quaint little woman on the committee named Miss Margaret Noe. Miss Noe was near eighty, and she was one of the few native Californians

I ever met in Los Angeles. She had been a school teacher for many years and was a delightful person. She loved the Lord, and she loved her church. And I shall never forget her telling me how she felt when the great James Fifield was minister of First Congregational Church. She said, "When he preached, heaven opened up for me. Afterward, I would go out into the garden in the church's atrium and sit on the edge of the fountain and just think about it. I never went up to speak to Dr. Fifield; I didn't want to break the spell. I just wanted to sit and dwell with the thoughts that had come to me." She was dwelling with God. When she came to church, she had an experience of worship.

The Wise Men came, they saw, they worshiped, and *they gave gifts*. Gold, frankinicense, and myrrh. Precious gifts. Not tawdry things, but the essence of all that was expensive.

Do you read the comic strip "Dennis the Menace"? In one strip, he and his mother and father were greeting the minister at the door after a service. Dennis said, "I thought it was a pretty good show for a quarter." The streaked lines across his father's face indicated embarrassment and humiliation.

A pretty good show for a quarter. That's often our attitude, isn't it? A gift is a little something in the offering plate, a tip for God. But the Wise

Men came and saw and worshiped and gave the best they could give.

Don't misunderstand. It isn't the size of the gift. It is the relationship of the gift to the resources of the giver. If we truly see and truly worship, we shall not be content to give God something minor and insignificant from our lives—the money we don't need or the time that is left over when we have done everything else. We shall want to give everything we have, to say, "Here, Lord, it is all Yours, I see that now. Let me return it to You, and have only enough left over to live on." Daily bread—that's what that phrase in the Lord's Prayer is about. Everything is God's, and we ask only for a little to live on.

Several months after Robert E. Lee ceased to be the great general of the Confederacy, he was offered the presidency of little Washington College in Lexington, Virginia. The school was bankrupt. Only forty students had been recruited for the next fall. Lexington was a remote little village, accessible only by canal boat on the river or by stagecoach over twisting, mountainous roads. But Lee regarded the invitation to be president as a call of Providence, and he accepted. Soon after he had moved to Lexington, important people from all over the country began making their way to Lexington to visit him. And before they left, they had pressed gifts of money and property on him for the school. They couldn't help themselves. In the presence of his greatness, they felt the need to give something. And, under their giving, the school flourished.

Isn't that the way it is when we see the Lord in worship? We see, and in our hearts we fall down before Him, and we want to give something—anything—everything—to the One who died for us and now stands at the center of all life and glory.

The Wise Men came and saw and worshiped and gave, and they set a pattern for us to follow all the days of our lives.

We have come, Lord; grant that we have seen. And, having seen, let us know what it is to have worshiped. And, finally, let us complete the cycle by giving ourselves in Your service. For You alone are and have the Word of eternal life. Amen.

45f MOTHER'S DAY !